"MAY ALL YOUR CONSEQUENCES BE HAPPY ONES."
—Bob Barker
Truth or Consequences

The TV GAME SHOW ALMANAC

John P. Holms
and
Ernest Wood

Chilton Book Company • Radnor, Pennsylvania

Published in Radnor, Pennsylvania 19089,
by Chilton Book Company

Designed by Robert Engle Design
Packaged by TD Media, Inc.; Tony Seidl, President
Manufactured in the United States of America

A CIP record for this book is available from The Library of Congress
ISBN 0–8019–8740–7

Photographs courtesy of PHOTOFEST

Thanks to all who helped make this book a game of its own.
Tony Seidl for putting it together.
Cyndi Maddox, Shannon Wickliffe, and Rick Anton for their fine research.
Robert Engle and Lorenz Skeeter for bringing it to life.
Jeff Day and Kathy Conover at Chilton for all their support and guidance.

And, special thanks to Leigh, who makes all things possible.

1 2 3 4 5 6 7 8 9 0   4 3 2 1 0 9 8 7 6 5

Contents

Introduction

An American Love Affair With The Correct Answer

Back in the late 1940s, when game shows were just beginning to appear on television, performer Fred Allen warned that this might not be such a good idea. "Giveaway programs," he said, "are the buzzards of radio."

Ever since, it's been a snap to find critics of the genre. "...The lowest form of television," says one. "...The most primitive and banal form of televised entertainment," declares another. "I can imagine no artifacts of popular culture more apparently worthless and seemingly unredeemed by any vestige of intellectual, aesthetic, or moral value...," opines a third.

But to put a game show spin on an old saying: If you're so smart, why ain't you come up with a better, more popular, more profitable kind of programming? Maybe the answer is simple. Maybe people like game shows because they're just plain fun!

Adults in the 1950s loved sweating along with Charles Van Doren in THE $64,000 QUESTION's isolation booth and although people were disappointed in his behavior, they eventually forgave him. Viewers laughed along with Art Linkletter on PEOPLE ARE FUNNY. College students in the 1960s were happy to put their knowledge to yet another test with Art Fleming and JEOPARDY! or try their hands at CONCENTRATION. For teenagers in the 1970s and 80s THE DATING GAME was a doorway to romance and PRESS YOUR LUCK kept them on the edge of their seats. Today it's AMERICAN GLADIATORS or an old favorite like FAMILY FEUD to give us our competitive edge.

And sometimes it seems like we've always been able to unwind after a hard day at work by watching Vanna White earn her keep flipping letters on WHEEL OF FORTUNE, or make the chores around the house a little easier with a little vicarious shopping spree on THE PRICE IS RIGHT. We even have a fledgling network devoted exclusively to game shows slowly coming on line.

These days we hear a lot about interactive television — shows that will let us talk back, shows that will let us participate, shows that will involve us as more than passive viewers. But it's funny, isn't that what game shows have been doing all along? The viewer who has never shouted out a price, the answer to a puzzle, or an arcane piece of trivia is the rare viewer indeed.

Which only makes us wonder if the past of television is also its future. It might be possible to soon say "I have seen the future and it's a game show." The critics and the cultural icons might not like it, but the rest of us are more then willing to roll the dice.

Good luck and keep your wits about you. What follows is an up-close look at the excitement and romance of the world of game shows and America's love affair with the correct answer.

John P. Holms
Ernest Wood
May 1995

How Can They Afford To Give All That Money Away, Mabel?

Part of the initial viewer fascination with THE $64,000 QUESTION lay in trying to figure out how the show could afford to shell out so much money in prizes. Here's the bottom line:

- Although actual production budgets were guarded like the crown jewels, best guesses in the trade were that the show was coming in at around $15,000 per week, including salaries paid to host Hal March, the live orchestra, camera crew and stagehands, and props, makeup, miscellaneous, and incidental expenses.
- In the first six weeks of the show just about $65,000 was passed out in prizes, for a rough average of $10,833 per week.
- That brings the show in at about $25,833 per week, very low for prime time television in the 1950s... and, therefore, very profitable.

Other top-ten shows were far more expensive (with the notable exception of other successful gamers):

- *The Jackie Gleason Show:* $72,500
- *The Milton Berle Show:* $90,000
- *The Jack Benny Show:* $42,500
- YOU BET YOUR LIFE: $35,000
- *The George Gobel Show:* $35,000
- Arthur Godfrey's *Talent Scouts*: $30,000
- I'VE GOT A SECRET: $22,500
- WHAT'S MY LINE?: $27,500

When you consider that the show was rated number 1 just four weeks after it launched and, therefore, charged top advertising dollar, it becomes clear that the producers and the network had a money machine on their hands. It's also pretty easy to figure out why the networks were clamoring for more and more of this extremely lucrative product.

A Brief History of TV Game Shows

50 Years of Fun and Games

"Let's hear it for Nabor from the other cave!"

There's been an argument raging in scientific circles for decades. It's one of the greatest unsolved mysteries in the history of man. Which came first: the quiz format or the stunt format? There was no videotape in the formative prehistoric years, and, so far, there's nothing on the cave walls to guide us. No one knows for sure, but we're going out on a limb and choosing quiz. The logic is simple. One of the first results of learning to talk was somebody asking somebody else a question, then another, and another. People gathered around and listened and cheered when somebody got the correct answer.

Mr. and Mrs. America and all their kids wait to catch Ralph Edwards and Truth or Consequences in 1950.

The next logical step involved giving a nice rock or a hunk of meat for a correct answer and the quiz show was born. Case closed. It follows then that the stunt format had to come along later as comic relief from sitting around the fire answering endless questions about the ancestors. In fact, there probably was a moment way back in deep B.C. when everybody was sitting around playing MANY QUESTIONS ABOUT THE TRIBE and the head guy said something like "I'm sorry, Ogg, but the answer was FIRE, so you're going to have to eat the whole snake standing on your head." This probably got a laugh and also drew more members to the next session and the headmen recognized the power of public spectacle to attract an audience. These sages became known as producers.

Maybe that's what happened, maybe not but...

The fact is that games have been played among family and friends for centuries to fill the evening hours, share a little fun, and maybe learn a little bit. Word games and simple stunt games were naturals because they were challenging, yet easy to play. The rules were simple and the games adapted themselves easily to the level of the players' skills. Also, they didn't require anything except people and a few things found around the house in order to play. "Parlor" games evolved and were refined over the years into sometimes challenging, sometimes silly, sometimes sophisticated, and yet always simple means of family entertainment. Twenty Questions, Dictionary, Hangman, and the like passed long winter nights for generations.

And that was basically the nature of game shows until the invention of the wireless radio brought the world into America's living rooms. Although quizzes and talent shows began to appear almost immediately, the date that game show madness was born is generally accepted as October 1, 1936, when a man named Craig Earl billed himself as PROFESSOR QUIZ and broadcast nationally from movie theaters across the country, bringing members of the audience up on stage between films to answer questions for cash. The gimmick caught on, and not only did PROFESSOR QUIZ spawn countless imitators, but he also insured a place for games shows on the major networks.

Radio filled our evenings with shows like INFORMATION PLEASE, QUIZ KIDS, TRUTH OR CONSEQUENCES, STOP THE MUSIC and the first big money game shows, POT O' GOLD and TAKE IT OR LEAVE IT (on which THE $64,000 QUESTION was based). Game shows had become a staple of radio even though they lost a little ground to more serious programming during WW II. But the concept was firmly established, and when the G.I.'s returned, so did the quizzes.

Television began to establish a national foothold in the years after the war with the evolution of the major networks. The execs were quick to realize that game shows could become a major programming element for reasons that went far beyond their popularity: they were cheap to produce. The low cost, studio-contained format was perfect for an industry beginning to flex its wings. As production technology advanced so did production values. What began as cloth-covered tables and answers written on blackboards for early shows like TWENTY QUESTIONS and WHAT'S MY LINE? would inevitably become the color, flashing neon, and glitz of WHEEL OF FORTUNE, JEOPARDY! and FAMILY FEUD. It's hard for a lot of us to remember that the fact of television in our homes in the 40s and 50s was spectacle enough, we didn't need bright colors to hold our attention and keep our fingers off the dial.

At any rate, Dumont, the first "major," began broadcasting nationally in April of 1946, and by June of that year, Demi James Sposa, aka Dennis James, had hosted the first episode of the first nationally televised game show, CASH AND CARRY. NBC, ABC, and CBS fell quickly into place. Game shows began to pop up like rabbits in a field. A ball had been set in motion that would continue to roll for the next 50 years.

By the 50s the radio biggies like YOU BET YOUR LIFE, TRUTH OR CONSEQUENCES, QUEEN FOR A DAY, and PEOPLE ARE FUNNY had all moved to TV, and the made-for-television institutions like BEAT THE CLOCK, WHAT'S MY LINE?, THE PRICE IS RIGHT, and PANTOMIME QUIZ had premiered. All carved strong positions in the ratings. The 50s introduced most of the enduring game show formats including panel shows, quiz shows, big-money shows, stunt shows, sob-story shows, couple-baiting shows and connection shows (see Glossary). The really big-money shows, THE $64,000 QUESTION and TWENTY-ONE, with their glamour and glitz came on the scene mid-decade and pushed the popularity of the genre over the top of the ratings mountain until the "Wizard of Quiz," Charles Van Doren, burst a national bubble. He caused a national crisis of conscience by admitting that he knew the answers to Jack Barry's questions before he walked into the isolation booth on TWENTY-ONE.

The decade of the 60s began with the question, "Are game shows dead on television forever?" The networks decided to excise the greed, go for the challenge, and see what happened. What they would eventually discover was that there was a direct connection between how much a contestant could amass and the shows' success. The issue was what they amassed and how they did it. There could be no hint of dirty doings in producers' offices. LET'S MAKE A DEAL was about bartering up to big-dollar merchandise and prizes. HOLLYWOOD SQUARES was up front. They admitted from the get-go that the panelists knew the answers in advance, which made it funnier. Chuck Barris said "to heck with prizes." He put ordinary folks in extraordinary situations on THE DATING GAME and THE NEWLYWED GAME and let them dig their own graves in public.

The 70s was a strange mix of reruns, retreads, insanity, and sex. Add "New" or "All New" to an old standard and give a proven performer another life—for instance, THE NEW PRICE IS RIGHT. Technology continued to make serious inroads with gigantic and complicated sets, flashing lights, and lots of loud noises on the gambling shows like HIGH ROLLERS and GAMBIT. "Chuckie Baby" Barris took the game show format right to the walls of the sanitarium with THE GONG SHOW and THE CHEAP SHOW. Hot sex and sneaky innuendo were the staples of THE NEW MATCH GAME and MINDREADERS. Jack Barry and Dan Enright, who had been brought low by TWENTY-ONE, rose out of the ashes like the mythical Phoenix and reintroduced big money to television with a revised version of TIC TAC DOUGH and a new one called THE JOKER'S WILD.

The 80s saw more money ($10,000 to $125,000) tagged onto some old standards and the networks reaped big profits (as in THE $50,000 PYRAMID). The decade was the beginning of a new movement in America, and people's taste was moving from kinky to conservative. Sex, at least on the networks, was pushed into the background by tradition and family values. But the real story was the incredible success of WHEEL OF FORTUNE and JEOPARDY! in syndication. The move to syndication realized huge profits for producer Merv Griffin and foreshadowed the decline of the networks' stranglehold on programming.

The 90s is a decade in search of a definition. The networks continue to produce the juggernauts like PRICE IS RIGHT and FAMILY FEUD. JEOPARDY! and WHEEL OF FORTUNE are bigger than ever in syndication. The phenomenal success of AMERICAN GLADIATORS says a lot about what we want to watch from the comfort of our living-room sofas. The cable networks are heavily in the game with reruns of old favorites, original entries, and children's games. State lotteries are also in the TV game show business. States like Ohio and California have adopted game show devices and formats to attract players. Even PBS has a game show hit in WHERE IN THE WORLD IS CARMEN SANDIEGO?

Where's it all going? Who knows. One thing we know for certain is that as long as a wheel is turning somewhere, people will gather to play and watch.

I Love Lucy Predicts the Future

The writers on *I Love Lucy* must have had some inside information or at least a crystal ball back in 1952. In a show called "Lucy Gets Ricky On The Radio" the team predicted the potential for rigging quizzes. Lucy and Ricky are listening to a game show called MR. AND MRS. QUIZ on the radio and Ricky knows all the answers. Lucy is amazed and enters them as a team on the show but Ricky gets furious and reveals he knew only because he was at the studio that afternoon during the taping. The only thing Ricky knows for sure is that "Columbus discovered Ohio in 1776." Lucy goes to the studio to get them off the show, but the producers like the idea of having a celeb on the air. What can Lucy do? She steals the answers and memorizes them. Of course they change the order of the questions and Lucy gets everything wrong. The *Lucy* episode #1050 aired May 19, 1952.

Todd Russell hosted the 1952 version of WHEEL OF FORTUNE which gave the recipients of good deeds the chance to repay their benefactors.

QUIZ 1: A BLAST FROM THE PAST

20 Questions from the Early Game Shows In Two Parts

Close your eyes for a second and imagine that you're in the old NBC studio waiting to go on as a contestant in one of the big-money, big-prize game shows of the '40s or '50s. Got it?

OK . . . OK . . . Now open them so you can read on and see how you would've done with this list of questions gleaned from some of the top game shows of yesteryear. Interesting to see what people wanted to know back then.

We've also included the prizes and cash that the victorious contestant carried home for knowing the right answer. If the rewards seem like big money even by today's standards; remember that $2,000 bought a lot of groceries in 1952 and it was easier to deal with the IRS. Lucky contestants really could "feather their nests" back then. But the clock is ticking and live television waits for nobody. It's almost your turn.

Here's an idea. Get a friend to be the host and ask you the questions.

There's the applause! See those huge cameras? The studio lights are hot. The red light's blinking... no pressure. Straighten your bow-tie or adjust the feather in your hat. Nervous? Why? There's only millions of people tuned in and they're all watching you.

Ready? Good, because your on!

Part One

1. **How many amendments are there to the Constitution?**
   You Bet Your Life   Cash Prize: $5,000

2. **You are climbing the famous Atlas Mountains. Name the continent you're on.**
   Strike It Rich $500

3. **What was the name of the plane which made the first nonstop flight around the globe in the spring of 1949?**
   Break the Bank $8,870

4. **What was the exact number of human beings on the ark during the 40-day deluge?**
   The Big Payoff   Mink Coat; Complete woman's wardrobe; Trip for two to stay anyplace in the world; Value: approximately $6,000

5. **Who was the French sculptor who created *The Thinker*?**
   You Bet Your Life $2,000

6. **In what year did Lincoln deliver his Gettysburg Address?**
   On Your Account $4,500

7. **"No stranger / to diamonds, / I've won a hero's crown, / think of several bills /and you'll find me, / now my tackle is winning renown. / who am I?"**
   Feather your Nest $2,500 in furniture

8. **In fifteen seconds: a) The first contestant will select a two-figure number, the other will substitute one digit from the other, as many as possible. b) Name as many occupations as you can that require a ladder. c) Give as many words as possible that end in "th."**
   Two For the Money $6,375

9. The real story of a man named Matt Evetic was made into a movie. It told how he risked death and suffered humiliation for his country. Name the movie.
   BREAK THE BANK $11,840

10. On May 28, 1934, The Dionne Quintuplets were born near a little town in Ontario, Canada. What town?
    YOU BET YOUR LIFE $1,500

Lightning Round

Now on your honor, would you recognize the tune, "The Girl in the Blue Dress"?

(answers on page 275)

Learning The Ropes

Just like children need training wheels on their first bikes, TV crews needed a little help in the beginning. The problem was that there weren't any big-deal schools of broadcasting around when television was in its infancy. ABC, for instance, wanted to be a brand new network in the late 40s, but was lacking a few of the necessary items to do that, such as a studio and people to run it if they had one. What was the fledgling network to do? Something that wouldn't have a snowball's chance in hell of happening today: they went to the biggies (notably that old softy Dumont) and asked to use Dumont's facilities to produce shows and gain experience for their crews. Dumont said "Sure!" and here are two early examples of how ABC learned to play the game:

PLAY THE GAME — Dumont 1946

(The show was actually produced by ABC)

QUIZZING THE NEWS — ABC 1948

The crews broadcast this current events quiz out of the competition's studios until their facility was open for business on August 8, 1948.

Maybe people were nicer in the old days.

Part Two

1. There is a time in the title of a famous 1950 movie which starred Gregory Peck as an air-base commander in England who was determined to win the war at all costs. What is the title?
   STRIKE IT RICH $500

2. "La Gioconda" is the original name of one of the most popular paintings in the world. What is the popular name?
   YOU BET YOUR LIFE $1,500

3. William H. Bonney was shot and killed by Sheriff Pat Garret. Who was Bonney?
   YOU BET YOUR LIFE $6,000

4. The Brooklyn Dodgers and the Boston Braves once battled for 26 innings, the longest game in modern major league baseball. It ended in a 1 to 1 tie. Two starting pitchers went the whole 26 innings. Who were they?
   BREAK THE BANK $9,900

5. What is the name of Shakespeare's famous clown in his plays "Henry IV" and "The Merry Wives of Windsor?"
   STRIKE IT RICH $500

6. In fifteen seconds: a) Give as many girls' names as possible beginning with the letters A, B, or C.
   b) Name as many animals as possible who normally climb trees.   c) Name as many living heavyweight champs as you can.
   TWO FOR THE MONEY $4,200

7. What was the food of the gods on Mount Olympus that insured them strength, power, beauty, and immortality?
   YOU BET YOUR LIFE $6,500

8. Name the war fought by the U.S. between 1802 and 1805 over payment of tribute.
   THE BIG PAYOFF $6,000

9. "I was a little fighter, / two islands are part of my / fame / my code wouldn't be righter, / Rip Van Winkle took part / of my name. / Who am I?"
   FEATHER YOUR NEST $1,350

10. An ancient country of Europe is south and west of the Rhine, west of the Alps, and north of the Pyrenees. The Celts were among its chief inhabitants. What's the name of this ancient country?
    THE BIG PAYOFF $10,000

Lightning Round

Now on your honor, would you recognize the tune, "The Navy and the Army, the Army and the Navy ?"

(answers on page 275)

It's No Mystery, Stupid — It's Latin!

The prize for the most intellectual game show title has to go to Q.E.D. (ABC 1951). Q.E.D. stands for *quod erat demonstrandum*, which means "that which is to be proven." Contestants tried to solve mysteries. Sometimes the show was called MYSTERY FILE, which is probably no mystery or at least less of a mystery than why it was called Q.E.D.

An Irony

Louis Cowan, producer of THE $64,000 QUESTION and president of CBS Television, who fell from grace after the quiz show scandals, died with his wife in a fire in their New York penthouse in 1976. The cause was said to be faulty wiring in the couple's television.

Fairy Tales Can Come True

When Allen Ludden was leaving as host of THE G.E. COLLEGE BOWL to go to PASSWORD, Robert Earle, who was working as a community-relations specialist with General Electric in Ithaca, N.Y., wanted the job. He was told by the producers to send a film of himself hosting a show. He'd never hosted a TV show, and thus didn't have any film. What he did was this: He audio taped a COLLEGE BOWL game, had the whole show transcribed into script form, went to an Ithaca radio station where he once worked and had Ludden's voice carefully edited from the audiotape. Then he went to WICB-TV, the Ithaca College station, set up a lectern in front of a camera, and ran a cord from a tape recorder with the edited tape in it to a foot pedal behind the lectern. With a camera rolling, he pretended to be hosting that COLLEGE BOWL game. He would ask the questions Ludden had asked (but which had been edited out), using the transcript, and then would step on the foot pedal to activate the tape to hear the students' responses. He did this with perfectly rehearsed precision to make it seem as if a BOWL session were going on, with him as host. He sent the film to the producers. He got the job.

A Gallery of Mystery Guests on What's My Line?:

Phil Rizzuto (WML's first guest)

Elliot Roosevelt (WML's second guest)

Duchess of Windsor (twice)

Eleanor Roosevelt

Carl Sandburg

Admiral Halsey

Chief Justice Warren
  (before Daly married his eldest daughter)

Frank Lloyd Wright

Marian Anderson

Liz Taylor (once at 17, once with Mike Todd)

Frank Sinatra

Gary Cooper

Bette Davis

Charlton Heston

Paul Newman

Woody Allen

Clint Eastwood

Lassie

Marlon Brando

The Hosts

The men behind the podiums and microphones.
(Their shows are listed in chronological order.)

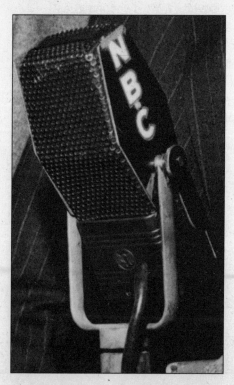

JACK BAILEY

If *People* magazine had been published in the 1940s and 50s, it would have named Jack Bailey "The Sexiest Man Alive." As host of QUEEN FOR A DAY for 20 years, Bailey became the prince of every housewife's Cinderella fantasy when he opened each show with: "Would YOU like to be Queen for a Day?" He debuted radio's QUEEN FOR A DAY in 1945 and, nine years later, made the transition to television. Bailey also emceed TRUTH OR CONSEQUENCES for two years. He started out in show business by acting in carnivals and tent shows. After the game show circuit, Bailey returned to acting with parts in several television series and performed in road shows of "Hello Dolly" and "How to Succeed in Business Without Really Trying." Bailey died in 1979.

Shows:

QUEEN FOR A DAY
PLACE THE FACE
TRUTH OR CONSEQUENCES

"The No. 1 mesmerizer of middle-aged females and most relentless dispenser of free washing machines."   *—TV Guide*

Jack Bailey and a host of beautiful models share a laugh before another segment of QUEEN FOR A DAY.

BOB BARKER

"I don't sing, I don't dance, I don't act, I don't tell jokes, and I'm not about to start now . . . because I'm a star." As the star host of The New Price Is Right, Bob Barker, along with sidekick Johnny Olson, made "C'mon down!" a part of the national jargon. With his reassuring voice and coolness under pressure—including the time a woman's breasts popped out of her tank top as she jumped up and down on contestants' row—Barker became a game show icon. Hearing Barker on the radio one night in 1956, Ralph Edwards hired the unknown Missouri disk jockey the next day to emcee TRUTH OR CONSEQUENCES. Barker became television's highest-paid game show host, earning $1.5 million from THE PRICE IS RIGHT in 1988.

Shows:

THE FAMILY GAME
THE PRICE IS RIGHT
TRUTH OR CONSEQUENCES

Master host Bob Barker and some of the essential elements for TRUTH OR CONSEQUENCES

"My job is to make other people funny. One of the highest compliments I've ever received was from an elderly woman on my show years ago. Afterward she wrote me a letter. 'Thank you so much for choosing me,' she said. 'You made me feel wonderful. In all my life, I have never been that funny.'"

W G M C
(World's Greatest Master of Ceremonies)

—A sign in Bob Barker's dressing room.

"He's like Leonard Bernstein. He conducts the audience as if it was his orchestra."

—Sammy Davis Jr., on Bob Barker

JACK BARRY

Better known as a game show packager, Barry began his working life as a handkerchief salesman and was host of the 1950s children's program *Winky Dink and You*. Barry hosted THE $100,000 BIG SURPRISE in 1955, but was fired after a year and replaced by Mike Wallace. However, he went on to become one of the most popular hosts of the 1950s, when he emceed and produced TWENTY-ONE—until the game rigging scandal revealed that it and another Barry production, TIC TAC DOUGH, were among the most rigged shows on television. Afterward, Barry struggled for 10 years to get back into the business, finally hitting a streak of luck again with THE JOKER'S WILD in 1972. Barry died in 1984, still the host of "JOKER".

Shows:

THE $100,000 BIG SURPRISE
JUVENILE JURY
LIFE BEGINS AT EIGHTY
TIC TAC DOUGH
TWENTY–ONE
HIGH LOW QUIZ
CONCENTRATION
THE GENERATION GAP
THE REEL GAME
THE JOKER'S WILD
BREAK THE BANK
JOKER! JOKER! JOKER!

"Whenever a contestant answers a question correctly, Jack's eyes pop out in astonishment, his mouth drops open, his face gets red, his hands begin to twitch."
—*TV Guide*

Host Jack Barry's return from game show purgatory after the TWENTY-ONE fiasco was with THE JOKER'S WILD.

"Dan (Enright) was the producer and Jack was the salesman. He could go to New York and sell a show in a minute. Dan would put a show together and then Jack would come in and watch us play the game in the office, and he would say what was wrong with it. He was a genius at looking at the end result and knowing what was wrong with it, and he was right 99 percent of the time."

—*Wink Martindale, game show host*

DICK CLARK

Known as "America's oldest teenager," Dick Clark may be best known as the charismatic host of *American Bandstand* (where game show producer-to-be Chuck Barris also worked), the annual New Year's Eve countdown from Times Square, and innumerable music-related programs. Over three generations, however, Clark has applied the energy of a young man to many forms of television, including game shows. After enduring a 1950s payola investigation of disk jockeys, he tried his hand, in 1963, as host of two short lived game shows. But a decade later, he applied his Midas touch to THE $10,000 PYRAMID. Known as a workaholic, Clark taped 15 episodes of PYRAMID in two days, every other week.

Shows:

THE OBJECT IS
MISSING LINKS
THE $10,000 ($20,000 $25,000 $50,000 $100,000) PYRAMID
THE KRYPTON FACTOR

By 1978 host Dick Clark
had given away over
$3,000,000 in prize money
on the PYRAMIDS.

CLAYTON "BUD" COLLYER

Bud Collyer planned to follow in his father's footsteps and become a lawyer. Instead, after two years of clerking, he turned to radio as the voices of Superman and Corporal Sheehan on *Renfrow of the Mounted*. The always-smiling Collyer hooked up with Goodson-Todman Productions on WINNER TAKE ALL and never left the company. He was the chief pie thrower on BEAT THE CLOCK and the mild-mannered emcee of TO TELL THE TRUTH. He claimed that during the 10-year run of BEAT THE CLOCK, he never met a bad sport. Devoutly religious, Collyer taught Sunday school every weekend in his hometown of Greenwich, Connecticut.

Shows:

MISSUS GOES A-SHOPPING
WINNER TAKE ALL
TALENT JACKPOT
BEAT THE CLOCK
BREAK THE BANK
MASQUERADE PARTY
ON YOUR WAY
FEATHER YOUR NEST
TO TELL THE TRUTH
NUMBER PLEASE?

"He was Mr. Affable, Mr. Big Smile, Mr. I Love You, How Are The Children? He never wore anything but a bow tie and ate six eggs for breakfast. Every morning."
—Gil Fates, executive producer of To Tell the Truth, on Bud Collyer

BILL CULLEN

With 24 shows to his credit, Cullen hosted more game shows than any other emcee in TV history. From the time he entered broadcasting at age 19 in 1944, he was never unemployed. At one point in the '60s, he simultaneously hosted shows on all three networks (THE PRICE IS

RIGHT on ABC, EYE GUESS on NBC and I'VE GOT A SECRET on CBS). Cullen was also a popular panelist on TO TELL THE TRUTH and I'VE GOT A SECRET. He began his career as a radio announcer in Pittsburgh and moved to CBS in 1944. Two years later, he was named emcee of Goodson-Todman's first radio show, WINNER TAKE ALL. By the 1980s, Cullen tried to retire from the business, but producers kept offering him new shows. Ironically, this most successful game show host almost wasn't hired for television because of a limp that resulted from a childhood bout with polio.

Shows:

ACT IT OUT
WINNER TAKE ALL
WHO'S THERE?
GIVE 'N TAKE
WHY?
WHERE WAS I?
PLACE THE FACE
BANK ON THE STARS
NAME THAT TUNE
THE PRICE IS RIGHT
I'VE GOT A SECRET
DOWN YOU GO
EYE GUESS
THREE ON A MATCH
WINNING STREAK
THE $ 20,000 PYRAMID
BLANKETY BLANKS
PASS THE BUCK
THE LOVE EXPERTS
CHAIN REACTIONS
BLOCKBUSTERS
CHILD'S PLAY
HOT POTATO
THE JOKER'S WILD!

Bill Cullen

"I'm happy if they win, and I'm upset if they lose. I am the timing, I am the pace. I speed it up. I play it down. I make it flow. It's a challenge."
—Bill Cullen

JOHN DALY

A respected CBS radio newsman who covered both the White House and foreign assignments, Daly ventured over to the entertainment side when Mark Goodson asked him to host WHAT'S MY LINE? for 13 weeks. Despite network policy forbidding news personnel from working for the entertainment division, Daly convinced management that the experience would help him learn more about television. CBS approved and he continued as host for the next 17 years. In 1953, while still hosting the show on CBS, Daly moved to ABC as vice-president of news and anchor of the network's evening newscast. A native of South Africa, Daly served as director of the Voice of America in the late 1960s and hosted a panel-discussion show on public television.

Shows:

WHAT'S MY LINE?
WE TAKE YOUR WORD
IT'S NEWS TO ME

"We picked him because he had great dignity and was a great ad-libber."
—Producer Mark Goodson, on choosing John Daly for What's My Line?

Quizmaster John Daly

RICHARD DAWSON

American audiences first saw the British-born Richard Dawson on their television screens as a wisecracking English POW on *Hogan's Heroes*. He also appeared on *The New Dick Van Dyke Show* and later as a regular on THE MATCH GAME — where he personally gave away more than $3 million. When FAMILY FEUD premiered with Dawson as its host, the loud, sometimes arrogant comedian sharply contrasted other game show hosts. When his kissing of female contestants drew criticism, he asked viewers to vote on the practice. The mail was 14,600 to 704 in his favor. Dawson who was host of FAMILY FEUD for its entire run, later returned to acting. His first role was as a smug and vicious game show host in the film adaptation of the Stephen King story *The Running Man*.

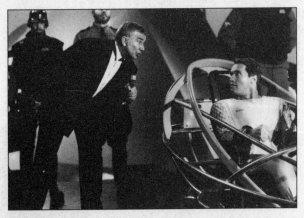

Richard Dawson of FAMILY FEUD fame appeared in 1987's *The Running Man* with Arnold himself as guess what? A game show host. Could this have been the genesis of AMERICAN GLADIATORS?

Shows:

MASQUERADE PARTY
FAMILY FEUD

"When contestants doze off, that's the thing that really ticks me off. And I tell 'em about it. But Bob Barker or those other guys won't do it because they all want to be Charlie Charming. They never really listen, anyway."

—*Richard Dawson*

HUGH DOWNS

Today's television audience knows Hugh Downs as the wise, grandfatherly counterpart to Barbara Walters on ABC's *20/20*. But Downs, like many other network newsmen, found fame on the game shows. He became a familiar face on television as a network announcer in Chicago with such shows as *Kukla, Fran & Ollie*. At NBC, he worked on *The Sid Caesar Show*. Downs was Jack Paar's sidekick on the original *Tonight Show*. Later, he doubled as host of *Today* (1962-71) and CONCENTRATION. He emerged from semi-retirement in 1978 to co-host the ABC newsmagazine, *20/20*.

Shows:

CONCENTRATION

Host Hugh Downs explains a rebus puzzle to assistant Patte Preble on CONCENTRATION, the show that replaced TWENTY-ONE. The puzzle? Con-cent-tray-shun. Maybe if she actually looked at the game board it'd be easier.

BOB EUBANKS

Bob Eubanks

If a skeleton was hiding in the closet or marital discord was brewing, Bob Eubanks was certain to expose it on THE NEWLYWED GAME. A concert and music promoter who booked the Beatles in Los Angeles and once managed Dolly Parton, Eubanks signed on to host Chuck Barris' hit game show in 1968. As emcee, he prompted newlywed couples to reveal their husbands' bizarre habits, their wives' shortcomings, and the "strangest places they ever made whoopee." Eubanks, an occasional rodeo rider, retired to a ranch outside Los Angeles.

Shows:

THE NEWLYWED GAME
ALL STAR SECRETS
RHYME AND REASON
THE DIAMOND HEAD GAME
DREAM HOUSE
TRIVIA TRAP
CARD SHARKS

ART FLEMING

As the host of JEOPARDY! for $12^{1}/_{2}$ years, Art Fleming became one of the most recognized men in the country. A suave and classy gentleman, he imparted trivia from such categories as religion, world geography and potpourri for 2,858 shows. Fleming started out as a radio announcer in North Carolina and eventually moved out to Hollywood. He enjoyed fame as the voice behind the

Art Fleming

commercial slogan, "Winston tastes good, like a cigarette should." While anchoring WNBC-TV's nightly news in 1964, he was spotted by Merv Griffin's wife, who urged her husband to hire him for the newly created JEOPARDY!. Later, he appeared on such television shows as *Starsky and Hutch*, and *Lou Grant* and in movies including *Primetime*, *Airport II* and *MacArthur*. Fleming died in 1995.

Shows:

JEOPARDY!
THE G.E. COLLEGE BOWL

MONTY HALL

Hoping to hit the big time after enjoying success as quizmaster and producer of the long-running WHO AM I? in his native Ontario, Hall decided to move to New York. There he found fill-in work on THE SKY'S THE LIMIT, VIDEO VILLAGE, and TWENTY-ONE. In 1963, along came the megahit LET'S MAKE A DEAL and Hall became known as the man who beckoned costumed contestants to choose from behind Door #1, Door #2, or Door #3. The popularity of Hall and his show was so great that when he moved it from NBC to ABC during a fee dispute in 1968, ratings for ABC's entire daytime schedule rose and NBC's dropped.

Shows:

THE SKY'S THE LIMIT
KEEP TALKING
VIDEO VILLAGE
LET'S MAKE A DEAL
IT'S ANYBODY'S GUESS
TWENTY-ONE
BEAT THE CLOCK
SPLIT SECOND

DENNIS JAMES

With the advent of television came Demi James Sposa, better known as Dennis James. The first TV host ever, he debuted on the Dumont Network's CASH AND CARRY in the 1940s. James' brother, Lou, worked as a technician for Dr. Allen B. Dumont, who was looking for a radio announcer interested in appearing on his planned television network. Lou suggested his brother, then working as a boxing announcer. James hosted a wrestling show—adding sound effects and humor—and was an announcer for "Ted Mack's Original Amateur Hour" before settling on games. Through 1975, James hosted 15 game shows, second only to Bill Cullen. He also made more than a half-million dollars a year as commercial spokesman for Kellogg's cereals and Old Gold cigarettes.

Shows:

CASH AND CARRY
THE NAME'S THE SAME
CHANCE OF A LIFETIME
TURN TO A FRIEND
JUDGE FOR YOURSELF
ON YOUR ACCOUNT
HIGH FINANCE
TWO FOR THE MONEY
HAGGIS BAGGIS
YOUR FIRST IMPRESSION
PEOPLE WILL TALK
P.D.Q.
CAN YOU TOP THIS?
THE PRICE IS RIGHT
NAME THAT TUNE

Dennis James and his wife Micki backstage, celebrating the 1st birthday of ON YOUR ACCOUNT (1955). Many think of James as the first game show host because CASH AND CARRY (1946) is considered the first nationally televised game show.

"[Contestants] weren't just pawns on a game show, they were real people to me. They had a great desire to win something, and I empathized with them."

—*Dennis James*

TOM KENNEDY

Game shows do get into your blood. A case in point: the Narz family. The brother of veteran game show host Jack Narz, Jim Narz used his older sibling's clout to leave Kentucky radio for Hollywood television. Once there, he changed his name to Tom Kennedy and landed his first job, on NBC's THE BIG GAME. Kennedy hosted 14 game shows, the most successful being NAME THAT TUNE. He holds third place among hosts with the most shows to their credit, behind Bill Cullen (24) and Dennis James (15).

Shows:

THE BIG GAME
DOCTOR I. Q.
YOU DON'T SAY
IT'S YOUR BET
SPLIT SECOND
NAME THAT TUNE
BREAK THE BANK
GRAND SLAM
TO SAY THE LEAST
WHEW!
PASSWORD PLUS
BODY LANGUAGE
THE PRICE IS RIGHT
WORDPLAY

Tom Kennedy.
The popular host is the brother of Jack Narz.

"NAME THAT TUNE *was the most exciting show I've ever done. We had a twelve-piece orchestra five feet behind us, and the audience was right out there. When you're in between the two of them, it's just electric."*
— Tom Kennedy

JIM LANGE

In 1965 Lange, a successful San Francisco disk jockey, began a 17-year commute from the Bay City to Los Angeles, the city he dubbed the "dating capital of the world." But he wasn't seeking a date for himself. He was host to the hot prime-time hit, THE DATING GAME. Chuck Barris spotted Lange as Tennessee Ernie Ford's sidekick on a television variety show. With Lange at the helm, THE DATING GAME aired both in the afternoon and on Saturday nights. Lange eventually moved to Los Angeles, where he continued working as a radio disk jockey.

Shows:

THE DATING GAME
GIVE 'N TAKE
SPIN OFF
HOLLYWOOD CONNECTION
BULLSEYE
NAME THAT TUNE
THE MILLION DOLLAR CHANCE OF A LIFETIME

ALLEN LUDDEN

A former school teacher who became known for his crew cut and horn-rimmed glasses, Allen Ludden endeared himself to television viewers as the amicable host of PASSWORD for a decade. He began his career in radio as director of programming for CBS, and served later as an executive of CBS News. Ludden sold his COLLEGE BOWL series to G.E. in 1953 and hosted BOWL and PASSWORD for the next 22 years. His first wife died a few weeks before he started on PASSWORD. Actress Betty White made a guest appearance on his third show, and she and Ludden married a year later. Ludden died in 1981.

Shows:

THE G.E. COLLEGE BOWL
PASSWORD
WIN WITH THE STARS

STUMPERS
THE LIAR'S CLUB
PASSWORD PLUS

HAL MARCH

Actor Hal March was well-known around Hollywood from his work in films, sitcoms and television variety shows when he emerged as the hottest emcee on the highest-rated game show of all times, THE $64,000 QUESTION. Executive Producer Steve Carlin noticed March on *The Imogene Coca Show* and promptly auditioned the handsome young actor. After the game show rigging scandal and the demise of QUESTION in 1958, March rarely worked again. He died of lung cancer at the age of 49.

Shows:

THE $64,000 QUESTION
WHAT'S IT FOR?
LAUGHS FOR SALE
IT'S YOUR BET

"I'm up there with these people. And I die when they don't know the answer. These others [game show hosts], they just select the contestants and get them onstage. Me, I've got to ask them the questions, have to live and die with them when I know as much as $64,000 is riding on their answers. I tell you, it's murder."

—Hal March

Standards Are Everything

John Daly, the newsman turned What's MY LINE? quizmaster and made it a national institution, resigned from *Critique*, a panel show on public television in 1969 after a panelist's remark that he considered obscene was not edited from the broadcast tape.

PETER MARSHALL

The original pilot for THE HOLLYWOOD SQUARES was shot with Bert Parks as host, but producers Merrill Heatter and Robert Quigley decided to replace him. Luckily for Peter Marshall, his photograph happened to be lying on a shelf at NBC. For 14 years and 5,000 episodes Marshall and SQUARES fit together hand-in-glove. As a former member of a vaudeville comedy team, Marshall possessed straight-man training that came in handy for "mastering" the comics who appeared on the show. After SQUARES, Marshall took up where he had left off, once again touring with theater roadshows.

Shows:

THE HOLLYWOOD SQUARES
THE STORYBOOK SQUARES
FANTASY
THE ALL STAR BLITZ

"Merrill [Heatter] made a game show host out of me."
—*Peter Marshall.*

WINSTON 'WINK' MARTINDALE

Growing up in Memphis, Wink Martindale knew Elvis Presley. He worked at the radio station where Presley cut "That's All Right Mama," his first record. But Martindale sought fame of his own, and like many others, Martindale headed west. After arriving in California in 1959 Martindale hosted a number of radio and TV music programs and game shows, then found what he had been searching for in the 1970s with GAMBIT and TIC TAC DOUGH. The two shows made a rich man of Martindale, who bought a lavish Malibu mansion and created his own game shows, including HEADLINE CHASERS and BUMPERSTUMPERS.

Shows:

WHAT'S THIS SONG?
DREAM GIRL OF 1967
HOW'S YOUR MOTHER IN LAW?
CAN YOU TOP THIS?
WORDS AND MUSIC
GAMBIT
TIC TAC DOUGH
HEADLINE CHASERS
HIGH ROLLERS

Wink Martindale

*"Wink gives you kind of a "Music Man" approach.
There's a performance. He's having a great time."*
—Merrill Heatter, producer of High Rollers

**Reaching Out to
The Mysterious East**

Gundy Worldwide, the syndicators of the venerable WHEEL OF FORTUNE and FAMILY FEUD are making plans to launch local versions of these Western staples in China, India, and Indonesia as well as in Japan, Hong Kong, and the Philippines. Local hosts and contestants will square off in local broadcast facilities. Wonder what the local Vannas will look like.

GROUCHO MARX

Despite the success of the Marx brothers' film and vaudeville career, Groucho Marx experienced a series of movie flops in the 1940s. He then tried his hand at radio, but without much success. Finally, at producer John Guedel's suggestion, Marx used his comedy and ad-libbing comic talents to host YOU BET YOUR LIFE. With Marx's trademark brash, biting sarcasm and familiar rumpled coat, cigar and broad mustache, the show became an instant hit, first on radio and again on the switch to TV in 1950. Though declared "washed up" only a short time earlier, Marx won an Emmy in 1950 as television's "Most Outstanding Personality." As host he created such popular phrases as "Say the secret word and win $100" and "Who's buried in Grant's tomb?"—a question that made certain than even losers left with $50.

Shows:

YOU BET YOUR LIFE
TELL IT TO GROUCHO

"The beauty of Jack Benny's humor is that he never pushes. I'm the antithesis of that, the wise guy, and it's the contestants who are in trouble."

—Groucho Marx

Groucho and George at the NBC mike. What else is there to say about perfection?

GARRY MOORE

In the 1950s, not many people could resist a guy in a crew cut and a bow-tie—especially when he was willing to wrestle an alligator on television or have a golf ball teed up and hit off his nose.

Garry Moore was another in a long line of game show hosts who began in radio, then switched to television. After several unsuccessful attempts to create a daytime variety show, he finally hit it big with a primetime quiz, the Goodson-Todman production, I'VE GOT A SECRET, which he hosted for 14 years. There, he could let his zany humor run free. (Moore did draw the line, however, at putting his head in a lion's mouth.) Six years later, he finally had a hit with his original ambi-

Garry Moore seems to be in need of his sponsor's product. Garry's zany humor made I'VE GOT A SECRET a national institution.

tion, *The Garry Moore Show*, a variety program that together with SECRET made him the highest-paid performer on television.

Show:

I'VE GOT A SECRET

JACK NARZ

Following the quiz scandals of the late 1950s Jack Narz was one of the few hosts to continue in the business. His show, DOTTO, was the first implicated for rigging games. Nothing indicated that Narz had anything to do with cheating, however. Afterward, Narz worked on TOP DOLLAR, SEVEN KEYS, and VIDEO VILLAGE. Radio fans first knew Narz in the early 1950s as bandleader Bob Crosby's sidekick and as the announcer on the children's show, *Space Patrol*. He moved to the game shows as announcer of QUEEN FOR A DAY. In the late 50s, Tom Kennedy (Jim Narz) followed his brother's footsteps to a successful career as a game show host.

Shows:

DOTTO
TOP DOLLAR
VIDEO VILLAGE
SEVEN KEYS
I'LL BET
BEAT THE CLOCK
CONCENTRATION
NOW YOU SEE IT

Hail To The Chiefs

Presidents Richard Nixon, Gerald Ford, Jimmy Carter and Ronald Reagan have all appeared on game shows: Reagan, first as an actor, then as governor on WHAT'S MY LINE?, I'VE GOT A SECRET, THE CELEBRITY GAME and others throughout the 50s, 60s, and 70s; Nixon, as VP on YOUR FIRST IMPRESSION, hosted by Monty Hall in the early 60s; Ford, as congressman in the 70s on WHAT'S MY LINE?; Carter, as governor in the 70s on WHAT'S MY LINE?

BERT PARKS

He was the all-American boy. Smiling, exuberant, a popular radio talent, and World War II veteran, Bert Parks became one of the industry's top hosts. Starting out at a radio station in Alabama, Parks advanced to CBS radio in New York at age 18. Following the war, he introduced his inimitable style as the singing and dancing emcee to a string of radio and television shows including, from 1950 to 1952, *The Bert Parks Show*. In the 1960s, Parks appeared in such Broadway productions as "The Music Man". Then he earned a spot in history as the host of *The Miss America Pageant* until pageant brass unceremoniously fired him for a more 'contemporary' emcee.

Shows:

BREAK THE BANK
STRIKE IT RICH
STOP THE MUSIC
BALANCE YOUR BUDGET
DOUBLE OR NOTHING
TWO IN LOVE
GIANT STEP
HOLD THAT NOTE
BID 'N BUY
THE BIG PAYOFF
MASQUERADE PARTY
YOURS FOR A SONG

Bert Parks sings a clue on STOP THE MUSIC.

"People criticize me. They dislike my effusive style, they think it's phony. They think it's impossible for anyone to smile that often. But it's not... There should be more bands playing and whistles going off."
—Bert Parks

GENE RAYBURN

The public first knew Gene Rayburn from the radio program *Rayburn and Finch*, four hours of comedy and music that ran from 1947 to 1953. Declining offers to go solo when he and partner Dee Finch split up, Rayburn hosted, instead, a children's show on WNBC, THE SKY'S THE LIMIT, and turned announcer for Steve Allen's *Tonight Show* from 1954-59. In 1962, Rayburn landed the host spot on THE MATCH GAME. The last of the New York school of game show hosts, Rayburn never moved west, preferring to commute from coast to coast.

Shows:

THE SKY'S THE LIMIT
MAKE THE CONNECTION
CHOOSE UP SIDES
TIC TAC DOUGH
DOUGH RE MI
PLAY YOUR HUNCH
THE MATCH GAME
SNAP JUDGMENT
THE AMATEUR'S GUIDE TO LOVE
THE MATCH GAME/HOLLYWOOD SQUARES HOUR
BREAK THE BANK

It's Economic

Why have television networks, syndicators — and now cable networks, been drawn to game shows? The answer is simple: they're cheap to produce. Sponsors donate prizes. Casts are small — except for contestants, who beat down the doors to appear for free. Profits from game shows have been estimated as high as 600 percent!

Did You Know That...

ONE HUNDRED GRAND—ABC 1963, was the first show to offer seriously big bucks after the heat from the rigging scandals had died down. You can bet that there were a lot of people looking over other people's shoulders. (But not for the answers, the questions were so difficult nobody had a chance anyway.)

PAT SAJAK

Where would the world be today without Pat Sajak and his lovely letter-turner, Vanna White? A former television weatherman in Los Angeles and Nashville, Sajak first became famous for cracking raw eggs on the pavement and watching them fry in the summer. That kind of antic got the attention of WHEEL OF FORTUNE producer Merv Griffin, who hired Sajak to replace Chuck Wollery. Even though he guided WHEEL into becoming one of the most popular game shows in history, Sajak considers himself a broadcaster, not a performer. In the early 1990s, Sajak tried his hand at late-night television, but his show never took off and was canceled within the season.

Show:

WHEEL OF FORTUNE

"As long as the 'Wheel' keeps spinning, everyone will live happily ever after!" —Merv Griffin, WHEEL OF FORTUNE producer

Dilla, You're a Killa

Groucho Marx thought that a housewife/contestant on YOU BET YOUR LIFE was so funny he gave her a push into show business. Her name? Phyllis Diller.

ALEX TREBEK

The dark, brooding looks of Alex Trebek became the standard for the new breed of 1970s hosts, nicknamed 'game show studs.' Another in a line of Canadians to hit the big time on American television, Trebek emigrated to host THE WIZARD OF ODDS, created by his friend and fellow Canadian, actor Alan Thicke. Known for his no-nonsense approach and strict adherence to the rules, Trebek reached superstar status in the 1980s as host of the revived JEOPARDY!. A 1994 poll of game show viewers rated him above all other hosts in every category, from honesty to sex appeal.

Shows:

THE WIZARD OF ODDS
HIGH ROLLERS
DOUBLE DARE
THE $128,000 QUESTION
BATTLESTARS
JEOPARDY!
CLASSIC CONCENTRATION

Alex Trebek

CHUCK WOLLERY

He wanted to be a country-music singer. Instead, everyone in the country knew Chuck Wollery as the host of WHEEL OF FORTUNE. Handsome and personable, like all good country-music singers, he was spotted by Merv Griffin while waiting backstage for a guest appearance on *The Tonight Show* in 1974. After seven successful years, Wollery quit spinning the wheel when Griffin refused him a $200,000 raise. Surely, there's a country music song somewhere in that story!

Shows:

WHEEL OF FORTUNE
THE LOVE CONNECTION
SCRABBLE

Chuck Wollery

Quiz 2: What's My Other Line?

4

Celebrity Hosts

The people who work in front of and behind the cameras hosting, announcing, assisting, appearing as panelists, modeling and the like come from many walks of life. Some of them are, were or became celebrities in other areas of public life. Get a pencil, concentrate and see if you can tag these game show celebs with their "other" occupations. It's not as easy as you think.

You'll find the answers listed on page 276

Host / Show	"Other" Occupation
1. **Mel Allen** JACKPOT BOWLING	_____
2. **Don Ameche** TAKE A CHANCE	_____
3. **Morey Amsterdam** BATTLE OF THE AGES	_____
4. **Jack Benny** THE BIG SURPRISE	_____
5. **Al Capp** ANYONE CAN WIN WHAT'S THE STORY? ANSWER YES OR NO	_____

6. **Johnny Carson** _____
   Earn Your Vacation
   Who Do You Trust?

7. **Clifton Fadiman** _____
   What's in a Word

8. **Joe Garagiola** _____
   He Said/She Said
   Joe Garagiola's Memory Game
   Sale of the Century
   To Tell The Truth

9. **Moss Hart** _____
   Answer Yes or No

10. **Ernie Kovacs** _____
    Time Will Tell
    Take A Good Look

11. **Gypsy Rose Lee** _____
    Think Fast

12. **Roger Price** _____
    Droodles

13. **Vincent Price** _____
    E.S.P.

14. **Basil Rathbone** _____
    Your Lucky Clue

15. **Bill Sterns** _____
    Are You Positive?

16. **John Cameron Swayzee** _____
    Chance for Romance

17. **Myron Wallace** _____
    Majority Rules

18. **Edgar Bergen** _____
    Do You Trust Your Wife?

A Real Head Turner

In 1961, as a joke, a friend of announcer George Fenneman came on YOU BET YOUR LIFE dressed as an Arabian prince. He won $10,000, which was no joke at all. When Groucho asked William Peter Blatty what he was going to do with the money, he replied that he was going to live off it while he wrote his book. The book turned out to be *The Exorcist*.

Two Little Bits Of Groucho

Woman contestant: "I have two locks of Elvis Presley's hair."
Groucho: "Do you have any cream cheese to go with it?"

Groucho: "How many children do you have?"
Contestant: "Thirteen."
Groucho: "I smoke a cigar, but sometimes I take it out of my mouth."

Somebody's Probably Got To Be First.

A CBS show with the politically incorrect name of MISSUS GOES A-SHOPPING is probably the first of a genre. Record keeping, however, was not a strong suit in the early days of the tube, so we'll never know for sure. This shopping for prizes entry started locally in New York in 1944 and went national in 1947. The host was John Reed King.

19. **Dick Butkus**
    STAR GAMES
    _____

20. **Bennett Cerf**
    WHAT'S MY LINE?
    _____

21. **Hans Conried**
    MADE IN AMERICA
    _____

22. **Leo Durocher**
    JACKPOT BOWLING
    _____

23. **Tennessee Ernie Ford**
    KOLLEGE OF MUSICAL KNOWLEDGE
    _____

24. **Bruce Jenner**
    STAR GAMES
    _____

25. **Bess Myerson**
    THE BIG PAYOFF
    _____

26. **Tom Poston**
    SPLIT PERSONALITY
    _____

27. **Carl Reiner**
    THE CELEBRITY GAME
    KEEP TALKING
    _____

28. **Jerry Van Dyke**
    PICTURE THIS
    _____

29. **Ben Vereen**
    YOU WRITE THE SONGS
    _____

30. **Flip Wilson**
    PEOPLE ARE FUNNY
    _____

31. **Stubby Kaye**
    SHENANIGANS
    _____

WINNERS...

The Most Influential and Important Game Shows of All Time

Since the first game show debuted on television in the fall of 1946 or maybe 1944, depending on your point of view, more than 400 different contests have been aired with varying degrees of success. What follows is an alphabetical look at the 51 shows that, for better or worse, have most influenced the world of game shows.

American Gladiators

Syndication   *1989–*

If BEAT THE CLOCK was a gentle mirror of the whimsical 50s, AMERICAN GLADIATORS is the in-your-face reflection of the 90s. It is the ultimate stunt/fantasy war game. Contestants, two men and two women, who have to be in excellent physical condition, go up against comic-book-style warriors, both male and female, in over-the-top battles on giant obstacle courses and suspended platforms. The warriors have names like Nitro, Malibu, Blaze, and Lace, and their costumes fit the names. But funny getups or not, these people aren't jokes. The games are tough and sometimes brutal. People occasionally get hurt in contests like Powerball, The Joust, Breakthrough and Conquer, and Hang Tough. The prize? $35,000 for making it through the entire sea-

Gladiator Zap gets a leg lock on a contender and tries to pull her from the rings in the Hang Tough segment of American Gladiators.

son. This is defiantly not about being able to balance a pie on a stick while you walk on a rail or how many balloons you can blow up in two minutes. Like the 90s, AMERICAN GLADIATORS is about survival.

Hosts:

MIKE ADAMLE
JOE THEISMANN
TODD CHRISTENSEN
LARRY CZONKA
REFEREE:
LARRY THOMPSON

Beat the Clock

CBS	1950–58
ABC	1958–61
Syndication	1969
CBS	1979–80

BEAT THE CLOCK spent a year on radio and moved quickly to television in 1950. The reason was simple: the show was all about zany stunts and watching was a whole lot more fun than listening. Contestants from the studio audience got the opportunity to make a little money or win a prize by doing things like pushing a 20-foot balloon through a small hole with two sticks, or trying to remove marshmallows from a bowl of jello with a spoon which was clamped in the contestant's teeth. This insanity, as well as stunts involving seltzer bottles, fire hoses, whipped cream, loud noises, and buckets of oatmeal, was invented by Frank Wayne, Bob Howard, and Neil and Danny Simon. As crazy as the stunts were, the producers insisted that contestants actually have a chance to pull them off so a staff of out-of-work actors, including soon to be anti-hero James Dean, was on hand as guinea pigs to try them out. BEAT THE CLOCK used over a thousand gallons of whipped cream in 1955. The financial remuneration for success wasn't important until the big-money game shows hit the air. After 1956 the reward for pulling off insanity could be as much as $64,000.

Hosts:

Bud Collyer
Jack Narz
Gene Wood
Monty Hall

Bud Collyer, host of BEAT THE CLOCK, waves good-by amidst a stuntsworth of broken cups and saucers.

The Big Payoff

NBC	*1952–53*
CBS	*1953–59*

In the 50s, the networks saw themselves as the guardians of the American family and the protectors of home and hearth. (Check out *Father Knows Best* and then take a look at *Married With Children* to see how far we've come.) Back then, even the game shows got in the act with contests that focused on hard-working and happy people making their way through the world together. To get on THE BIG PAYOFF, contented husbands wrote letters to the producers explaining why the women they married were special beyond fabulous and therefore deserving of the "Big Payoff" because they were so great. The chosen hubbie came on the show to answer a series of questions that became more detailed and difficult. If he hung in there he won jewelry, fur coats, and clothes for the perfect one in his life and a brand new car for his personal dedication, commitment, and intelligence. The really big payoff was a trip anywhere in the world via Pan Am for him and his deserving mate. The show also included segments called the "Big Little Payoff" for children and "Turn About Payoff" so the wife could return the favor. Bess Myerson was the hostess with the mostess.

Hosts:

RANDY MERRIMAN
BERT PARKS
MORT LAWRENCE
ROBERT PAIGE

The Big Surprise

NBC   *1955–57*

After The $64,000 QUESTION went through the ratings ceiling, everyone was looking to compete with a big-money game show. As usual, the producers sought gimmicks and high-concept to separate their efforts from the rest of the herd (and to acheive a hit). "SURPRISE" was no exception. Among the hooks tried during the early months of the show were rescuing a contestant who missed an answer by having someone else answer a different question. Rescued contestants had to give up 10% of their winnings. Contestants were given the choice of "easy" or "hard" questions. Easy questions that were missed resulted in the loss of all winnings. Misses on hard questions cost only half. Eventually the producers realized that the audience was primarily interested in watching people struggle and sweat to win big money. They simplified the game considerably making the contestants answer a series of questions toward a top prize of $100,000. The only gimmick that continued from the early days was that contestants could answer an "insurance" question at any point in the round and guarantee all their winnings up to that point. The show was doing well until the rigging scandals made the networks retreat from anything that smelled of fixing and big money.

Hosts:

JACK BARRY
MIKE WALLACE

Did You Know That...

Dick Clark made his first trip off the bandstand in 1963 to host an ABC show called THE OBJECT IS.

Break the Bank

ABC	*1948–49*
NBC	*1949–52*
CBS	*1952–53*
NBC	*1953*
ABC	*1954–56*
NBC	*1956–57*
ABC	*1976*
Syndication	*1976–77*
	1985–86

BREAK THE BANK was a blockbuster on radio and made the transition to television with ease. Always a big-money show, contestants could work their way through a series of progressively more difficult and lucrative questions until they got a chance to BREAK THE BANK and win several thousand dollars depending on how long it had been since someone else had broken it. Viewers wrote postcards which were placed in the Wish Bowl. They hoped to become the "Wish Bowl Couple" and receive an all-expense trip to New York to compete on the show. When the show went to really big money in 1956, studio-audience contestants were replaced by experts who competed for a top prize of $250,000. (Which, as far as we know, no one ever actually won.)

Hosts:

BERT PARKS
TOM KENNEDY
JACK BARRY
GENE RAYBURN
JOE FARAGO

Cash and Carry

DUMONT 1946–47

CASH AND CARRY was probably the first game show broadcast over network television, which premiered on June 20, 1946. The problem is that accurate records weren't kept in the early days of television so it just isn't known for sure when a lot of local shows crossed the network bridge. CASH AND CARRY's chief competition for the record is a CBS show with the same shopping-in-a-supermarket format called MISSUS GOES A-SHOPPING and it was hosted by James Reed King. CASH AND CARRY was set in a grocery store and the shelves were lined with the sponsor's (Libby's) products . The shopper/contestant chose items from the shelves and by answering the questions attached to them could win cash prizes ranging from $5 to $15. Of course, winners also got to keep the merchandise. Just to spice up the action, the studio audience participated in silly stunts involving pantomime or action guaranteed to make a mess, such as eating pudding blindfolded with the hands tied behind the back. The original (and only host) Dennis James got the job and the start of a television career because his brother worked for Dumont in the Jersey labs.

Host:

DENNIS JAMES

Did You Know That....

Host Dennis James's real name was Demi James Sposa.

Concentration

NBC   1958–73
Syndication   1973–79

CONCENTRATION was pushed on the air as a temporary replacement for the soon-to-be-tarnished TWENTY-ONE. Jack Barry was the original host but he lasted only 4 shows before his association with the scandal made him too hot to handle. His bad luck was Hugh Downs good fortune because the show took off and became a major success for NBC, lasting almost 15 years and syndicating for 6 more. The format was based on a children's game. Contestants looked at a board with 30 squares. Behind each square was a prize. Each player in turn tried to pick two squares that contained matching prizes. Matches added the prize to the player's list. Misses meant that the squares reverted to blanks, and it was up to the players to remember where possible matches were positioned on the board. The only way to keep all the prizes accumulated during play, however, was to guess the answer to the rebus puzzle that was revealed as items were matched. The action was fast and furious, and as a bonus the audience could play along at home, having just as much fun as the contestants. They wouldn't get the loot, but they could always feel smarter than the folks who made it on the air.

Hosts:

JACK BARRY
HUGH DOWNS
BOB CLAYTON
ART JAMES
ED MCMAHON
BILL MAZER
JACK NARZ
ALEX TREBEK

The Cross-Wits

Syndication   1974–80
                  1986–87

A slick and sophisticated crossword puzzle game in which two teams, each with a member of the audience and a celebrity, competed to complete a crossword puzzle using clues provided by the host. Points were awarded for each correct entry. The winning contestant then needed to fill in ten words during a 60-second "Crossfire" in order to win a trip to an exotic foreign city. Winners were allowed to choose the celebrity they felt would be of the most help in completing the "Crossfire." Some of the great and near-great who helped fill in the blanks were Alice Ghostley, Jo Ann Worley and Vicki Lawrence.

Hosts:

JACK CLARK
DAVID SPARKS

The Dating Game

ABC   1965–73
Syndication 1974–75
               1977–80
               1986–89

A pretty, perky young woman interviewed three unseen bachelors and then had to decide which one she would go out with on a date. The dates, which were sponsored by the show, were usually to some exotic or unusual spot. The questions, which seemed to come from the "bache-

A couple finds happiness on THE DATING GAME.

lorette," were actually written by the show's staff and were geared to elicit spicy exchanges. The show has had several reincarnations including THE NEW DATING GAME and THE ALL NEW DATING GAME. It was based on BLIND DATE an early gamer with America's first female hostess, Arlene Francis. The clones of THE DATING GAME have gotten more and more risqué and full of pretty upfront sexual content. STUDS, for instance, leaves little room for doubt as to the nature of its programming content and concept.

Hosts:

JIM LANGE
ELAINE JOYCE
JEFF MCGREGOR

Do You Trust Your Wife?

CBS	*1956–57*	
ABC	*1957–63*	*(Daytime)*

Perhaps the first in the spouse-baiting for laughs genre, this show asked husbands to decide whether or not their wives would try to answer a question on a specific topic. The jackpot for winner's was $100 a week for a year. The gimmick and the laughs came from ventriloquist Edgar Bergen and his famous trio of dummies—Charlie McCarthy, Mortimer Snerd, and Effie Klinker,—as they questioned and made fun of the husband and wife teams. Johnny Carson and Ed McMahon took over when the show went to daytime. Ed was the only sidekick in television history to replace a bunch of dummies. Well, on second thought...

Hosts:

EDGAR BERGEN
JOHNNY CARSON
WOODY WOODBURY

Dollar a Second

DUMONT	*1953–54*
NBC	*1954*
ABC	*1954–55*
NBC	*1955*
ABC	*1956*
NBC	*1957*

Host, Jan Murray of DOLLAR A SECOND and a willing contestant.

Contestants began winning money the moment they stepped in front of the studio audience. They were paid a dollar for every second they were on the show and a dollar for every correct answer to some strange and wacky questions. When they were wrong they were penalized and had to perform a stunt designed to get some surefire laughs from the audience and the viewers at home. Contestants could stop at any time and collect their winnings because, just like in life, certain things were out of their control. For each show, the producers designated an "outside event," such as when a train might pull into Grand Central Station or a bathtub would overflow. If the event occurred while the contestants were on the air, they lost everything. The outside event was monitored by the audience but not the players. The producers of game shows were among the first in the industry to recognize and exploit the emerging technology of television.

Host:

JAN MURRAY

Down You Go

DUMONT	*1951–55*
CBS	*1955*
ABC	*1955–56*
NBC	*1956*

This show is a classic because of its simplicity and its trust that the charm and wit of the celebrity panelists would make for great viewing. The format was simplicity itself—take the children's game of hangman and have the likes of Boris Karloff, Jayne Mansfield, Arthur Treacher, Jean Kerr, Francis Coughlin, Phyllis Cerf, and Phil Rizutto play it. This fascinating mix of famous people from vastly different walks of life were given clues by host, and actual English professor, Dr. Bergen Evans. The panel competed to guess the phrase, letter by letter, as revealed on what was called the "magic board." The show spawned a board game that retained some popularity even after the show

Down You Go's host, Dr. Bergen Evans with panelists Carmelita Pope and Toni Gilman.

was off the air. The panelists played for fun, but viewers were paid $5 if a phrase they sent in was used and the hefty sum of $25 if they were able to stump the stars. Nobody got rich playing Down You Go , but for five years everyone had a grand old time.

Hosts:

DR. BERGEN EVANS
BILL CULLEN

Family Feud

ABC   1976–85
Syndication   1977–85
                   1988–

This one was and is a biggie. Two teams of families compete by guessing how the studio audience has responded to questions in a poll, for instance, "name the most popular vacation spot on the East Coast." Englishman Richard Dawson became famous for provoking internecine strife during his lengthy interviews of each family before the actual game and for getting kisses from the ladies who competed. His wit and charm were a big reason for the show's popularity and it's no surprise that he returned to the helm several years later to bolster sagging ratings. The producers could win a prize for the most convoluted title of a spin-off when they came up with THE NEW FAMILY FEUD CHALLENGE. (Just a personal opinion.)

Hosts:

RICHARD DAWSON
RAY COMBS

Richard Dawson and contestants on the set of FAMILY FEUD.

The G.E. College Bowl

CBS	1959–63
NBC	1963–70
Syndication	1978–79

Even before pro football clogged the airwaves on Sunday afternoons, there was a fiercely competitive sporting event to gather around the tube to watch. It was called THE G.E. COLLEGE BOWL. Lots of sweat and effort, but as far as we know—never any mud or blood. Just tough, grind'em out Q & A. But boy, it could be exciting. During its 11-year run, the show never lost its charm or appeal and continued to draw strong audiences. Two teams of four, each representing their college's best and brightest, squared off against one another and the clock. The team amassing the most points won scholarship money for their college and the right to return the following week. A five-time winner won a trophy. The questions were tough and the teams were truly challenged. COLLEGE BOWL was intelligent, exciting, heart-warming, and fulfilling, since the fresh-faced youngsters competed only for the joy of knowledge and to be of aid to the old school.

Two men of Brown and two women from its sister college Pembroke prepare for battle with Northwestern University on January 24, 1958.

Hosts:

ALLEN LUDDEN
ROBERT EARLE
ART FLEMING

The Gong Show

NBC   *1976–78*
Syndication   *1976–80*
                    1988–89

THE GONG SHOW put Chuck Barris on the map; and, while you can't really call this bad talent contest a game show, it's such a mythic fixture in the audience participation genre that it's just got to be included. The worst in amateur talent competed to be the best of the worst. The show was a classic in semi-controlled bad taste. Acts were judged by a wacky and rambunctious panel that included J.P. Morgan, Jamie Farr, Rex Reed, Phyllis Diller, Arte Johnson, Rip Taylor, Steve Garvey, Ken Norton, and Dr. Joyce Brothers. The panel could gong contestants off the stage at any time. Some were removed so quickly that a minimum time was established just to be fair. (Why they bothered, we don't know.) Some of the acts were so weird and strange that they became fixtures (such as the Unknown Comic with the paper bag on his head) and returned over and over again for heaps of abuse. The prize for win-

ners was a "golden gong" plus $712.05 for the evening show or $516.32 for daytime. The prizes were based on AFTRA (the television performers union) minimum day rates for actors.

The Bait Brothers go for the gusto on THE GONG SHOW. This act proved beyond a doubt that two heads aren't necessarily better than one.

Hosts:

GARY OWENS
CHUCK BARRIS
DON BLEU

High Rollers

NBC	*1974–76*
	1980
Syndication	*1976–77*
	1987

As a reward for correctly answering a progressive series of questions, winning contestants were given the opportunity to roll some large dice in a variety of games to win cash prizes and merchandise. The show was noted for its emphasis on Las Vegas glitz and glamour and for its high-rolling hosts—two of the most popular in the business.

Hosts:

ALEX TREBEK
WINK MARTINDALE

The Hollywood Squares

NBC	*1966–80*	*(Daytime)*
	1968	*(Prime Time)*
Syndication	*1971–82*	
	1986–89	

Nine celebrities sat in a three-storied tic-tac-toe board graced with bright lights and lots of neon. The host asked general-interest questions, which the celebrities answered in as entertaining a fashion as possible. Contestants had to determine whether the answer was right, wrong, or a bluff. If the contestants were right, they got an X or an O on the board. The first contestant who accomplished tic-tac-toe with three adjacent symbols won the game, receiving cash and prizes. With celebrities like Paul Lynde, Joan Rivers, Jonathan Winters, and Wally Cox answering the questions, the contestants often took second fiddle to the jokes and wacky answers. The producers eventually decided to script some of the ad-libs to keep the laughs rolling in. It was a smart move because the success of the show was really based on the wit and humor of the panel members as opposed to the intelligence of the contestants.

Hosts:

PETER MARSHALL
JON BAUMAN
JOHN DAVIDSON

An early publicity still for HOLLYWOOD SQUARES.
(*clockwise bottom left to right*) Host Peter Marshall, Rose Marie,
Wally Cox, Morey Amsterdam, and a mystery personality.

I've Got a Secret

CBS	*1952–66*
	1976
Syndication	*1972–73*

For a show that was to become one of the classics of the genre, I'VE GOT A SECRET was a horse that barely made it out of the starting gate. The initial broadcast found the audience in a courtroom with host Garry Moore dressed as a judge while the panelists, pretending to be lawyers, questioned contestants seated in a dock. It was silly. Good sense prevailed, however, and what the audience found on tuning in the second time around was the simple panel format which would drive this little gem to become one of the most successful game shows ever. And it was so simple: the contestants had a secret that four panelists had to fathom. The audience, which was flashed the secret via the marvelous technology of television, watched as the panel struggled to dig out the answer with clever and effective questioning. The chemistry of the panel that rivaled WHAT'S MY LINE? for wit and humor included, over the years, Harry Morgan, Eddie Bracken, Orson Bean, Kitty Carlisle, Betsy Palmer, and Bess Myerson.

Hosts:

GARRY MOORE
STEVE ALLEN
BILL CULLEN

Cristiano did this sketch of the I'VE GOT A SECRET team to celebrate the 10th Anniversary and 490th show in 1962. The group includes host Garry Moore, and left to right, Bill Cullen, Betsy Palmer, Henry Morgan, and Bess Myerson.

Jeopardy!

NBC	1964–75
	1978–79
Syndication	1974–75
	1984–

Instead of giving answers to questions, players hear the answers and give the questions. Six categories, each containing six answers are put into play for each round. The dollar value of each answer is progressive, as is its difficulty. Because the contestants' money is always at risk, the tension level on JEOPARDY! is one of the highest in gamedom. The "Double Jeopardy!" round, where players can risk all their earnings on a single answer, can make a winner out of a loser. The pace is so relentless and fast, the viewers at home can play with a sense of urgency and commitment that doesn't require a cash prize to break a sweat. From the beginning, producer Merv Griffin insisted that the level of questions be difficult and demanding; and sticking with that choice has made JEOPARDY! a blockbuster and an American institution.

Hosts:

ART FLEMING
ALEX TREBEK

Juvenile Jury

NBC	1947–53
CBS	1954–55
Syndication	1970–71

Smart producers have always known that children can make for great television and great ratings. This was apparent with Jack Barry's JUVENILE JURY. The panel, in this charming and often hilarious show, consisted of five children ranging in age from three to twelve, who were asked to come up with solutions to "problems" sent in by viewers. Announcer Jack Barry, who created the show for radio and transferred it to television, picked his panelists carefully, and the result was a group of uninhibited and quick-thinking young wordsmiths and phrasemakers. The show was live, and so whatever came out of the children's mouths went over the airwaves. This could normally strike terror into the heart of a network censor, but because they were innocents, all could be forgiven when something was a little risqué. Barry was a master at getting the best out of his little jurors. He once asked a little girl what she wanted to be when she grew up. "A doctor," she replied. "Why?" he asked. "Because I like to stick needles in people, " she answered with a smile. The syndicated version lacked some of the charm of the original, perhaps because children seemed to grow up a little faster in the turbulent 70s.

Host:

JACK BARRY

Kay Kyser's Kollege of Musical Knowledge

NBC   1949–50
                       1954

Bandleader "Professor" Kay Kyser, dressed in cap and gown, was the zany host of a musical quiz noted much more for its insanity than its content. Musical questions, acted out by a resident company and

KAY KYSER'S KOLLEGE OF MUSICAL
KNOWLEDGE was as wacky as they come.

members of the band (dressed in college sweaters and wearing beanies), were posed to members of the studio audience who did their best to answer them. A panel of three strange men dressed in tails and wearing beards sat at a table and "judged" the correctness of the answer. Some memorable early TV comedians participated in the show, including the famous vaudevillian Ish Kabibble. Kay Kyser was a wild man in the Spike Jones tradition and the "KOLLEGE" was a truly wacky place to study. It probably could have had a significant life had it not run into conflict with its sponsor. The show was shut down in 1950 but reopened briefly in 1954 with Tennessee Ernie Ford as host.

Hosts:

KAY KYSER
TENNESSEE ERNIE FORD

Lets Make A Deal!

NBC	*1963–68*
ABC	*1968–76*
Syndication	*1984–86*

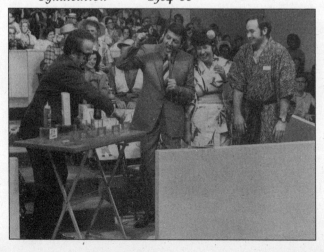

Monty Hall in high gear during first round play on LET'S MAKE A DEAL.

Monty Hall chose contestants from the studio audience (all of whom came in silly costumes to attract his attention) and offered to make a deal to trade something they brought with them for a prize. That prize could then be traded for something else. The something else, however, was concealed and, therefore, unknown. You had to trade something you knew for something you didn't. The sticker was that the unknown prize could be anything from a rotten apple to a diamond ring. If contestants could control their greed level and continue to trade for objects of increasing value (in other words, not get "zonked" and lose everything), they were eligible for the "big deal of the day" which involved picking what was behind one of the three famous curtains or doors. The prize could be a trip to Paris or a pen and pencil set. The fascination lay in watching traders go through the sweaty and gut-wrenching process of deciding whether or not a bird in the hand is worth two in the bush. A young man named Bob Hilton hosted the show briefly in syndication but was dropped when it became clear that only Monty could really make the deal.

Hosts:

MONTY HALL
BOB HILTON

Life Begins At Eighty

NBC	1950
ABC	1950–51
DUMONT	1952–55
ABC	1955–56

The appeal of this spin-off of JUVENILE JURY is evident in the fact that it ran for over six years. A panel of wise and clever gray-hairs from all walks of life answered questions submitted by viewers and by the studio audience and got a chance to give life the perspective of years. Everyone was actually over 80, and over the course of the show's run several passed away. Two regulars, Fred Stein and Georgiana Carhart, were with the show from the beginning and were well into their 90s when it went off the air. Producer/creator Barry included a segment called "Footlight Favorites" during which aging performers got a chance to strut their stuff.

Host:

JACK BARRY

Masquerade Party

NBC	*1952*
CBS	*1953–54*
ABC	*1954–56*
NBC	*1957*
CBS	*1958*
NBC	*1958–59*
CBS	*1959–60*
NBC	*1960*
Syndication	*1974–75*

The rich and famous and the great and near-great disguised themselves in truly elaborate costumes and makeup and appeared before the trusty panel whose job it was to guess their identities. The disguises were

The one and only MASQUERADE PARTY. It's interesting to note the meager (by today's standards) production values. The focus was clearly on the wit and charm of the panelists and the guests.

clues to who they were in real life. Once again, the technology of television aided the celebrities in their deception: the microphones they used were scrambled to disguise their famous voices. Money earned from stumping the panel went to charity. The show was fast and funny, making MASQUERADE PARTY very popular television during its nine-year run. The format was clearly more durable than the regulars, however, because seven hosts and over 19 regular panelists, including Ogden Nash, Dagmar, Betsy Palmer, Jonathan Winters, Audrey Meadows, and Pat Carroll, moved through the show during its stint on the air.

Hosts:

BUD COLLYER
DOUGLAS EDWARDS
EDDIE BRACKEN
ROBERT Q. LEWIS
BERT PARKS
RICHARD DAWSON
PETER DONALD

The Match Game

NBC	1962–69
CBS	1973–79
Syndication	1976–81

A panel of celebrities was asked a question such as "name a part of a chicken." Regular contestants then had to match celebrity answers for rewards of cash and merchandise. Later versions had the celebrities and contestants fill in the blanks, as in "John put his *blank* in the water." The questions provided plenty of opportunity for double meanings and a lot of funny answers. The evening version, called MATCH GAME P.M., took the double-entendre to far greater lengths; six racy panelists and two willing contestants dealt with fairly explicit material (for television at that time anyway). The show was very popular, both on network and in syndication, doing quite well for its sponsors and the careers of its panelists, including, Richard Dawson, Brett Sommers, and Charles Nelson Reilly.

Host:

GENE RAYBURN

Name That Tune

NBC	1954	(Summer)
CBS	1954–59	(Fall)
NBC	1974–75	
Syndication	1974–81	
	1984–85	

In the longest-running guess-the-song quiz, band leader Harry Salter had his orchestra play a song until one of the contestants recognized it, raced 25 feet across the stage, slapped a loud and obnoxious buzzer, and "named that tune." The contestant with the best knowledge of music and the strongest legs went on to the jackpot round at the end of the show and had a chance to win $1,000 in the viewer selected "Golden Medley." It wasn't easy. The winner had to name seven songs in 30 seconds. As the show progressed into the 70s and 80s, the jackpots rose with inflation to as much as $100,000, but you still only had to run 25 feet. No Pressure.

NAME THAT TUNE with a contestant (*left*) and host, George DeWitt. Note the famous bell and rope above and the "high-tech" timing device in the background.

Hosts:

RED BENSON
BILL CULLEN
GEORGE DE WITT
RICHARD HAYES
DENNIS JAMES
TOM KENNEDY
JIM LANGE

The Name's the Same

ABC   1951–55

The hook on this one was very simple. Based on the tried and true success of What's My Line?, it would, in turn, influence I'VE GOT A SECRET. A panel of celebrities questioned guests, who had the same name as a famous person, place, or thing such as Abe Lincoln, Mona Lisa, Mr. Rushmore, or A. Spoon. The celebrities' job was to guess his, her or its identity. Some of the regular panelists, who were the life of this particular party, were Abe Burrows, Audrey Meadows, Gene Rayburn, Carl Reiner, Mike Wallace, and Basil Rathbone.

Hosts:

ROBERT Q. LEWIS
DENNIS JAMES
BOB (ELLIOT) AND RAY (GOULDING)
CLIFTON FADIMAN

The Newlywed Game

ABC   1966–74
Syndication   1977–80
                     1988–

The combination of newlyweds and money resulted in some classic television moments. The game was simple: 4 newly-married couples competed as teams. They were separated and asked to guess how their partners would answer a list of questions that presented numerous possibilities for misunderstanding and fireworks, such as "How often is your husband in the mood?" The all-time winner for an off-the-cuff misunderstanding of a leading question has to have been the classic from The New Newlywed Game in 1987:

Eubanks: "Where will your husband say is the strangest place the two of you have ever made whoopee?"

Female contestant: "In the butt, Bob!"

In the weeks following the famous blooper Eubanks guessed that he could have sold millions of "In the Butt" T-shirts.

Host:
_____

Bob Eubanks

Pantomime Quiz (aka Stump the Stars)

CBS	1949–51
NBC	1952
CBS	1952–53
DUMONT	1953–54
CBS	1954
ABC	1955
CBS	1955–57
ABC	1958–59
CBS	1962–63

In the first, and still champion, of the celebrity-charade genre, two teams of celebrities played charades using material suggested by viewers. The show was always waiting in the wings as a summer replacement in the days when networks really had seasons that began in the fall and ended in the spring. That's what accounted for its network jumping-bean act and for its longevity. The show was a lot of

Vincent Price, one of the PANTOMIME QUIZ "home team"
plays charades with Hans Conreid, Adele Jergens, and
ex-child-star, Jackie Coogan. The year was 1951.

fun, and, like THE HOLLYWOOD SQUARES it enticed a long and distin-
guished line of celebrity contestants Vincent Price, Hans Conreid,
Jackie Coogan, John Barrymore, Jr., Carol Burnett, Dick Van Dyke,
Stubby Kaye, Elaine Stritch, Rocky Graziano, and Milt Kamen, to
name a few.

Hosts:

MIKE STOKEY
PAT HARRINGTON, JR.

Password

CBS	1961–67	
ABC	1971–75	(PASSWORD ALL–STARS)
NBC	1979–82	(PASSWORD PLUS)
	1984–	(SUPER PASSWORD)

Two teams, each composed of a celeb and a contestant, used word association to get a partner to say the "password" using the least number of clues. Only single-word clues were allowed, no hand gestures or phrases. The value of a correct answer went down by a point with each incorrect response to a clue. The no-hand rule led to some serious wiggling and squirming as contestants struggled to remain physically calm but quick and clear. The winners went to the "Lightning Round" during which they had a chance to win cash and the right to return by associating five passwords in 60 seconds. PASSWORD was a brilliant concept, and the game succeeds on the two most important counts: It's fun to watch and fun to play. The board game has always been a major seller.

Hosts:

ALLEN LUDDEN
TOM KENNEDY
BERT CONVY

People Are Funny

NBC	1942–61	(Radio)
	1954–61	
	1984	

Before he went into radio and television, John Guedel worked as a writer for Laurel and Hardy. The combination of slapstick and human drama so integral to the work of that brilliant comic duo led him to

On a Hollywood street Larry Bomer, PEOPLE ARE FUNNY's 20,000th guest, starts hitching a ride to Fort Worth, Texas where he will try to cash a check for $1000 written on a 135 pound watermelon. If he succeeds he gets to keep the money. Art's not going with him.

wonder what could happen if a stunt show could go for laughs and still touch a human chord. He came up with PEOPLE ARE FUNNY. In Art Linkletter he found the perfect host. Always a shrewd judge of people, Linkletter had the ability to push his contestants to hilarious heights without humiliating them. PEOPLE ARE FUNNY focused on how people dealt with bizarre situations. For instance, a man who thought he was taking a bath in his Los Angeles hotel room but was actually in a semi-trailer which was moved by crane and revealed to the public on the corner of Sunset and Vine. The show was all in fun and the good natured contestants walked away with a Hoover vacuum cleaner for their efforts.

The writers and creative team were so savvy that the concepts for several segments eventually became hit shows. Without PEOPLE ARE FUNNY's "Detecto" would there have been To TELL THE TRUTH? Without "Think Alike" would there have been the THE NEWLYWED GAME? "What's My Occupation?" foreshadowed WHAT'S MY LINE? and "What's In The Box?" laid the foundation for LET'S MAKE A DEAL.

As they say, imitation is the sincerest form of flattery.

Host:

ART *"People are funny, you know...and we're going to prove it"* LINKLETTER

The Price Is Right

NBC	*1956–63*
ABC	*1963–64*
Syndication	*1972–79*
CBS	*1986–*

THE PRICE IS RIGHT is a juggernaught, consistently high in the ratings and making mincemeat of the opposition in whatever time slot it happens to be in. The game is played by four contestants who compete with each other to come closest to the actual retail price of a selected piece of merchandise. The task is to be close without going over. The popularity of the game is based on fast action, furious pace, and serious competition for expensive items. THE PRICE IS RIGHT succeeds in making guessing retail feel like gambling. The new version relies on video and a group of approximately 60 different pricing games. The beat goes on five days a week on CBS.

Quiz master Bill Cullen on the original PRICE IS RIGHT SET.

Hosts:

BILL CULLEN	DENNIS JAMES
BOB BARKER	TOM KENNEDY
BOB BARKER	

Queen for a Day

NBC	*1945–59*	*(Radio)*
ABC	*1956–64*	
Syndication	*1970*	

The hook that will push a game show into the stratosphere can come from anywhere and anything—especially desperation. Producer Ray Morgan needed bodies in the seats for a forgettable morning radio show. He couldn't lower the ticket prices because the show was free so he came up with the next best thing. He started giving away flowers to lure women into the audience. It worked. It seemed to make them feel, as Jack Bailey later put it, "... like they were Queen for a day." Morgan wondered what it would take to make the average woman feel like a Queen. He decided that solving her most pressing problem in front of a studio audience might be the answer. The rest is game show history. When it was all over, 5,000 ladies had been given over $23 million in prizes for having the saddest and sometimes strangest stories on television.

It worked like this. Four needy women told Jack Bailey their wishes and then presented a tale of woe such as "My husband needs a new artificial eye because last winter his froze and cracked." The presentations may have had some unexpected humor, but the needs were real and it was each contestant's job to persuade the audience to crown her "Queen for a Day." A lot of tears flowed on the stage and in the audience. The famous applause meter decided all, and the winner was granted her wish along with a wardrobe, appliances, home furnishings, and, of course, a bouquet of roses.

Hosts:

JACK BAILEY
DICK CURTIS

Quiz Kids

NBC	*1949–52*
CBS	*1952–53*
	1956
Syndication	*1978*
	1990–91

QUIZ KIDS was the grandaddy of them all, beginning on the radio in 1940. Several bright, all-American youngsters answered some really tough questions that tested general and specific knowledge. Ironically, the original host, a man by the name of Joe Kelly, hadn't gotten past the third grade. The kids stayed on the show as long they maintained a winning average of correct answers or until they turned 16. The participants actually were smart, each contestant being an expert in a specific area, such as math; but they were expected to dredge up answers to queries in general fields as well. One of the kids, Robert Strom, whose specialty was astronomy, made it to the big leagues and won a small fortune on THE $64,000 QUESTION and THE $64,000 CHALLENGE answering questions on the stock market. When the show returned for a year in 1956, a man of recognized intellect was seated in the host's chair—Clifton Fadiman. It reappeared in 1978 under the QUIZ KIDS banner and again in 1990 as THE QUIZ KIDS CHALLENGE.

Hosts:

JOE KELLY
CLIFTON FADIMAN
JIM MCKRELL
JONATHAN PRINCE

Little Lonnie Lunde is ready to answer a question on the ever popular QUIZ KIDS.

The $64,000 Question/The $64,000 Challenge

CBS   *1955–58*
Syndication   *1976-78*

On THE $64,000 QUESTION contestants tested their knowledge of specific subjects in rounds of play that grew progressively more difficult and larger in value. The players were placed in high-tech isolation booths. Winners stayed as long as they wished and could quit with their earnings at any time or risk it all for more money. The show was an instant success and became the highest-rated game show in television history.

Marine Captain Richard McCutchen and his father John, are about to become the first $64,000 winners. They knew the seven courses served at a dinner at Buckingham Palace in 1939. Host Hal March listens intently.

On THE $64,000 CHALLENGE winners from "QUESTION" were brought to compete against each other on a higher level for more money. Two contestants, each in an isolation booth, could both attempt to answer the questions, with the loser being forced to leave. However, if both missed, both continued. Over the years the shows gave away a lot of Cadillacs as consolation prizes and more than a million dollars to the winners. The highest single cash prize was awarded to a postal clerk from St. Louis named Teddy Nadler who claimed to have memorized an entire encyclopedia. He proved it and won $252,000. Child stars Patty Duke and Eddie Hodges both won $8,000 on "CHALLENGE".

However, it was alleged that some of the contestants were fed answers by the producers. When the Dotto rigging scandal leaked out in 1958 and TWENTY-ONE was nailed for cheating, the big-money game shows collapsed under their own weight. Eventually it came out under investigation that, unlike what happened on TWENTY-ONE, the producers of "QUESTION" and "CHALLENGE" did not give the contestants answers. Instead they tested, trained and interviewed contestants to determine what kinds of things they knew and tailored the questions to exploit that knowledge. Several contestants revealed that questions used in training sessions were asked on the show.

The same show concept reappeared in syndication as THE $128,000 QUESTION and ran from 1976 to 1978.

Hosts:

HAL MARCH (THE $64,000 QUESTION)
SONNY FOX (THE $64,000 CHALLENGE)
RALPH STORY (THE $64,000 CHALLENGE)
ALEX TREBEK (THE $128,000 QUESTION)

Split Second

ABC   1972–75
Syndication   1986

A Q & A game with every American's dream at the end of the rainbow: a brand new car. Each show began with Tom or Monty touting five fabulous automobiles which were displayed around the stage. People picked from the studio audience answered general-knowledge questions to try to win one. Triumphant contestants were given a key to one of five cars. If the key fit the car the contestants picked, it was theirs; if not, they could come back and try to win another chance. The cars remained on the show until the right key fit the right ignition. The fantasy of getting a dream machine for free made for some genuine excitement opportunities, and there was usually a lot of shrieking and sweaty palms while the winners tried out their chosen keys.

Hosts:

TOM KENNEDY
MONTY HALL

Stop the Music!

ABC   1949–52
                    1954–56

Another spawner of spin-offs, STOP THE MUSIC! was the first of the musical quiz shows on television. A big-band leader named Harry Salter played a musical recognition game with his audience as part of his touring act in the 30s and 40s. The gimmick was very successful and Salter realized that it was a natural for television. He came up with the idea of having his orchestra and singer/host Bert Parks perform snatches of a melody until one of the contestants recognized the tune, screamed "stop the music," and named it for cash and prizes. Salter went on to develop and produce a spin-off called NAME THAT TUNE that became the long-running hit he had hoped STOP THE MUSIC! would be.

Host:

BERT PARKS

Strike It Rich

CBS	*1951–55*
Syndication	*1973*
	1978
	1986–87*

STRIKE IT RICH was perhaps the most controversial game show ever aired on network television. To qualify, contestants had to be in terrible trouble—due to unemployment, illness, injury, or some other horrible twist of fate—and need money desperately in order to bail themselves out. On the show they would tell their tales of woe and answer some simple questions in return for money. Even if they missed the answers they could appeal to viewers on the "Heart Line" phone for contributions so everyone walked away a "winner."

There were hundreds of cases of people hiking and hitching to the CBS studios in New York just to try to get on the air. Many were stranded on the streets of Manhattan

Host Warren Hull and singer Kitty Allen of STRIKE IT RICH sort through the "Heartline To America" mail to select the lucky few worthy of the phone call that could be worth a $500 Savings Bond.

when they were turned away. A storm of protest rose around the show with charities and good-will organizations pointing out that of the thousands of applicants, only a very few could get on the air so the show catered more to voyeurism and exploitation than to good works. Others, however, saw it as a high-minded and noble achievement and applauded CBS's humanitarian efforts.

Hosts:

WARREN HULL
BERT PARKS
TOM KELLY
JOE GARAGIOLA*
When the show returned in 1986 it returned in name only with Joe Garagiola hosting a straight Q & A format.

The $10,000 Pyramid

CBS	1973–74	
ABC	1974–76	
ABC	1976–80	(THE $20,000 PYRAMID)
Syndicated	1974–1979	(THE $25,000 PYRAMID)
CBS	1982	(THE $25,000 PYRAMID)
Syndicated	1981	(THE $50,000 PYRAMID)
	1985	(THE $100,000 PYRAMID)

Like PASSWORD, the PYRAMID family of contests was a word association game. The difference was that teams, consisting of a celebrity and a contestant, could use gestures, signals, and phrases to help each other guess the object word. However, in the "Winner's Circle," which was the big-money part of the game, nothing other than one-word clues were allowed as the contestants attempted to guess 6 categories in 60 seconds. No wonder the winners felt like jumping when they pulled it off.

Hosts:

DICK CLARK
BILL CULLEN

Susan Richardson of *Eight is Enough*
congratulates a junior champion on
THE $20,000 PYRAMID in 1979.

To Tell the Truth

CBS	*1956–68*
Syndication	*1969–78*
NBC	*1990*

There were three contestants in each segment of this famous show.
They were all introduced as the same person and it was up to a panel
of celebrities to question each one and determine who were lying and
who was telling the truth. Once the panelists wrote down their guess-

Garry Moore and the contestants on the revised To TELL THE TRUTH set.

es, Bud Collyer intoned the now famous "Will the real _____ please stand up." The contestants split the money for the wrong guesses. The panelists included Polly Bergen, Hy Gardner, Kitty Carlisle, Ralph Bellamy, Tom Poston, Orson Bean, Peggy Cass and Hildy Parks. For many of them including Kitty and Peggy To TELL THE TRUTH was as close to a permanent job as there is on television. The genesis of To TELL THE TRUTH was the "Detecto" segment on Art Linkletter's PEOPLE ARE FUNNY.

Hosts:

BUD COLLYER
GARRY MOORE
JOE GARAGIOLA
ROBIN WARD
GORDON ELLIOT
LYNN SWANN

Treasure Hunt

ABC	*1956–57*	
NBC	*1957–58*	
Syndicated	*1973–76*	(THE NEW TREASURE HUNT)

Contestant teams, composed of a man and a woman, answered a series of questions worth $50 apiece. The winners of the question round got the chance to go on a "treasure hunt" which involved picking one of several treasure chests. A "pirate girl" hostess, dressed in revealing type gear, opened it to show what was inside. The treasure could be anything from a loaf of bread to a check for $25,000. When Chuck Barris reissued the show in syndication in 1973 he, as usual, cut to the chase eliminating the Q & A and pitting the two contestants against each other to pick the chest with the big bucks inside.

Hosts:

JAN MURRAY
GEOFF EDWARDS

Truth or Consequences

NBC	*1940–50*	*(Radio)*
CBS	*1950–51*	
NBC	*1954–65*	*(Includes daytime)*
Syndication	*1966–74*	
	1977–78	

TRUTH OR CONSEQUENCES, the first of the "stunt" shows, had a 10-year run on radio before its move to television in 1950. Ralph Edwards, an announcer with "Major Bowe's Amateur Hour," invented the game based on the children's game forfeit, in which one player has to guess the identity of another or perform a stunt. In 1940, TRUTH OR CONSEQUENCES debuted on NBC, and Edwards posed questions such as "Does a hen sit or set when she lays an egg?"

Contestants were given an impossibly short time to answer before "Beulah the Buzzer" cut them off, forcing them to attempt a silly and impossible stunt. Edwards and a zany staff continually invented new stunts and had the biggest radio game of the 1940s.

With Edwards as host, TRUTH OR CONSEQUENCES won an Emmy its first year on television, but the move was not easy. As a CBS program, the show was switched from prime time to daytime, offered (but had no winners for) prizes as large as $100,000 and broadcast live from Hot Springs, New Mexico, after the town took up a challenge to change its name to Truth or Consequences. The show was a technical leader, too, using three cameras for coverage earlier than any other. Edwards, however, was busy with another new venture, "This Is Your Life," and the show lasted only one season.

In 1954, TRUTH OR CONSEQUENCES returned to NBC, hosted for two years by Jack Bailey, emcee of QUEEN FOR A DAY. Then in 1956, Edwards auditioned a young announcer he'd heard while listening to his car radio. The fellow's name was Bob Barker. Edwards offered him the job, Barker accepted and remained with the show on network and in syndication until 1974. Barker refined the format with outrageous costumes, a chimpanzee named Beulah, embarrassing skits, and elaborate stunts that sometimes ended in sentimental reunions with relatives. "Consequences" could take as long as a week to complete, requiring contestants to return for another show.

A syndicated show in 1977 and 1978 was hosted by Bob Hilton, and a brief but forgettable 1987 version was emceed by comic Larry Anderson, with assistant Murray (the Unknown Comic) Langston.

From radio through syndication, TRUTH OR CONSEQUENCES ran 37 years—longer than any other game show in broadcasting history.

Hosts:

RALPH EDWARDS
JACK BAILEY
STEVE DUNNE
BOB BARKER
BOB HILTON
LARRY ANDERSON

Twenty-One

NBC   *1956–58*

When word began to leak that TWENTY–ONE was rigged, no one could believe it. When it turned out to be the case, the scandal rocked the game show world and created a moral crisis in America. The show itself was a variation of the casino card game,

The moment of truth. Vivenne Nearing unseats Charles Van Doren on TWENTY–ONE. Host Jack Barry delivers the question.

Blackjack. Contestants gathered points (from 1 to 11 per question) for correct answers, seeking to reach the magical total of 21 before their opponent. The potential winnings were huge—the largest dollar amount, $220,500, was won by Elfrida Von Nardroff. The show was extremely successful due to the intellectual prowess and charisma of its contestants and America set its clock to soak up the excitement and dream about winning big money. It turned out that the producers were making sure that the contestants appeared bright and attractive by hand selecting them and giving them the answers in advance. A "winner" named Herb Stemple, angry that the producers asked him to take a dive because he was losing viewer support, blew the whistle when he was replaced by Charles Van Doren. Van Doren ultimately confessed to cheating after winning more than $140,000 and the scandal that followed signaled the end of the magical 50s. Even President Ike, who was a big game show fan, called the sorry mess worse than when the Chicago Black Sox fixed the World Series at the turn of the century.

(See: 10. The End of Innocence)

Host:
_____

JACK BARRY

Mr. Van Doren's Stats
(He had it all)

As quiz champion on TWENTY–ONE, Charles Van Doren:
- Won $129,000.
- Received 2,000 letters a week.
- Attracted 500 proposals of marriage.
- Appeared on the cover of *Time* magazine.
- Was named summer host on NBC's *Today* program (at $1,000 per week).
- Increased sales of Geritol by 40 percent.

Twenty Questions

NBC	*1949*
ABC	*1950–51*
DUMONT	*1951–54*
ABC	*1954–55*

TWENTY QUESTIONS deserves a nod as a top game show because it followed the format of the classic and enduring parlor game of the same name and translated it perfectly to television. Panelists were given 20 yes or no questions to deduce the identity of an object. Just as in thousands of American living rooms and taverns, the first question was always "Is it animal, mineral, or vegetable?" The pace was fast and lively, and the panelists were always funny and quick.

Hosts:

BILL SLATER
JAY JACKSON

The TWENTY QUESTIONS panel does their magic
on the Dumont Network.

Video Village

CBS   1960–62

Though VIDEO VILLAGE had a short summer run on CBS, it wins awards for inventiveness and originality. Using the emerging technology of television, the show became a living board game for the contestants, who moved from square to square by rolling a giant die in a cage. The giant board was a fictitious village and the host and his assistants were the mayor and his officials. The announcer was called the town crier. Each square offered a prize, a move, a reversal or a question to be answered for cash or penalty. The winner got the opportunity to continue play with a new challenger. Other game shows were used as formats for successful board games. VIDEO VILLAGE turned the tables by starting with a board game format and then becoming a best-selling board game for Milton Bradley.

Hosts:

JACK NARZ
MONTY HALL

What's My Line?

CBS   1950–67
Syndication   1968–75

Eighteen years is a long time for anything. For a prime-time television show it is unheard of. For a prime-time television game show it's darn near impossible; but as they say, it's in the books. WHAT'S MY LINE? had an 18-year prime-time run and was one of the most recognizable shows on television. The success was not due to the cleverness of the game but to the cleverness and wit of the panelists. Their job was to question contestants and determine their occupations. The contestants got $5 every time they could answer "no," and 10 nays

WHAT'S MY LINE? panelists Arlene Francis, Ernie Kovacs,
Dorothy Kilgallen, and Bennett Cerf along with host John Daly
(*standing*) have good reason to smile. The show's a big hit.

meant they won. The regulars were some of the best minds on television and included Arlene Francis, Dorothy Kilgallen, Louis
Untermeyer, Hal Block, Bennett Cerf, Steve Allen, and Fred Allen.
Untermeyer, a poet and critic, was accused of being a communist and
was blacklisted during the McCarthy hearings. The charges were
unfounded but he was banned from television. While appearing on
the show Steve Allen coined the now-famous eliminator question "Is
it bigger than a breadbox?"

Hosts:

JOHN DALY
WALLY BRUNER
LARRY BLYDEN

Wheel Of Fortune

NBC   *1975–91*
Syndication   *1983–*

Pat and Vanna celebrate the 3000th spinning of the Wheel. "It's an easy game," says Vanna, "everyone of all ages can play and enjoy at the same time. A two-year-old can sit and enjoy watching the wheel spin. I get all kinds of letters from people saying their child learned the alphabet from watching the show."

When TV execs get new jobs they like to start from scratch with their own lineup of shows. That's exactly what happened when Lin Bolen became head of daytime programming for NBC in 1974. One of the first things she did was contact Merv Griffin about buying out the balance of his JEOPARDY! contract and replacing it with his new show called SHOPPER'S BAZAAR. Griffin was ready. He had already done two pilot episodes, one with Chuck Wollery and one with Edd "Kookie" Byrnes of *77 Sunset Strip* fame.

The pilots were both shot on a set that had the look of an exclusive Beverly Hills boutique with lavish gifts and prizes displayed in a lush retail atmosphere. Winners would visit the fancy shop after the game and select their prizes. The original spinning wheel was a huge vertical affair with the usual bells and whistles.

Once the new show was a go from Bolin and NBC, Griffin rethought the game and simplified the set, eliminating the boutique. Other major conceptual alterations were to make the wheel horizontal and, of course, change the name of the show. The results made everyone very happy.

Wollery was chosen over Byrnes and hosted for several years before he left the show over a salary dispute with Griffin. Sajak replaced him and is still at the helm today. WHEEL OF FORTUNE started on NBC and moved to syndication in 1983. It remained on the network, however, until 1991. Sajak hosted both versions until he began his short-lived syndicated talk show in 1989.

WHEEL OF FORTUNE is one of the most highly rated syndicated programs in television history and a phenomenon of the 70s, 80s, and 90s. The object is simple. Contestants spin the wheel and raise money to buy letters on the puzzle board. They try to guess the mystery word or phrase by filling in the letters as they earn cash or prizes. Vanna turns the letters and models the furs. We're all winners when we watch the wheel of fortune spin!

Hosts & Hostesses:

CHUCK WOLLERY
BOB GOEN (NBC DAYTIME 1990)
PAT SAJAK
VANNA WHITE
SUSAN STAFFORD

Winner Take All

CBS	1948–50
NBC	1951–52

WINNER TAKE ALL was a veritable hotbed of television firsts. It was the first Goodson-Todman production for television, the first to have contestants use a buzzer or a bell to signal they were ready to answer a question instead of screaming something at the top of their lungs, and the first to have contestants continue on the show as long as they continued to win. Two contestants went head to head on general knowledge questions. A right answer was worth a point and the first to acquire three points was a winner. On the daytime version actors also performed skits and song-and-dance numbers. As was usual at the time, the commercials were live and done by the actors and the host.

Host:

BUD COLLYER

You Bet Your Life

NBC	1950–61

The focus of this immensely popular game show wasn't the game or the contestants, it was the wit and humor of Captain Spaulding himself, Groucho Marx. The other elements essential to the show's success were the announcer, George Fenneman, and, of course, the duck that came down to announce the secret word. At the beginning of each show Fenneman told the audience the secret word. The contestants were then introduced and interviewed at their own risk by Groucho. Eventually they were asked some questions and they had to agree on the answer before reporting it to the cigar. If, during their time on stage, the contestants said the secret word, they were immediately rewarded with $100. Even if contestants failed to answer any question correctly, there was always the consolation round where they would have to determine something such as who was buried in Grant's tomb. As far as we know, that question was answered correctly almost every time.

As the show entered its final season in 1961, it was renamed THE GROUCHO SHOW and the duck was replaced with dancing girls and the occasional gorilla. In the 80s Buddy Hackett took a shot at the format as did Bill Cosby in the 90s but, as they say, there's only one Groucho.

Host:

GROUCHO MARX

April 18, 1956 marked the date that Groucho attempted to replace the famous YOU BET YOUR LIFE Duck with Marylin Burtis as the conveyor of the "secret word." Although the duck carried a bomb and Marylin had only boxing gloves she evidently managed a draw because she appeared occasionally as the barer of good news.

You Don't Say

NBC   *1963–69*
ABC   *1975*
Syndication   *1978–79*

A team made up of a celebrity and a contestant worked together to guess the name of a famous person. One was given the name and had to help the other guess. The tag line for the show was "It's not what you say that counts, it's what you don't say." YOU DON'T SAY was vintage hosting by the always popular Tom Kennedy, brother of Jack Narz.

Host:

TOM KENNEDY
JIM PECK

You're In The Picture

CBS   *1961*

The execs in the suites at corporate must have believed the creatives when they said that the combo of Jackie Gleason and a game show was a natural.

"How would it work?" corporate asked the day the show was pitched.

"Listen to this," the creatives said, "We get these cardboard cutouts like at Coney Island. You stick your head in the hole, and you're a body builder or a cowboy or something, and you get your picture taken. We get four celebrities to stick their heads in the holes. But here's the hook: the celebrities have to guess what they're doing in the cutout scene. And, get this, Jackie gets to be funny while they're trying to figure it out. What do you think?"

"We trust you guys. If you think it's funny, let's do it," the corporate types said.

And it came to pass that people were hired, money was spent, and YOU'RE IN THE PICTURE went before the cameras January 20, 1961, with high hopes and great expectations.

The show was canceled after one broadcast because no one, least of all The Great One, was interested in watching panelists try to guess the nature of the cardboard cutout they were sticking their heads through. YOU'RE IN THE PICTURE was a complete disaster.

It's a safe bet that corporate was looking for places to put blame and that some creative head rolled down the carpeted halls of the Columbia Broadcasting System on January 21st. The price for failure is high and executives never make mistakes.

Host:

JACKIE GLEASON
(who went on the air the following week
to cancel the show in person)

Space For Your Personal Top Ten List of the
Best Game Shows Ever

1. _____

2. _____

3. _____

4. _____

5. _____

6. _____

7. _____

8. _____

9. _____

10. _____

6

The Scariest, Strangest, Weirdest, and Worst Game Shows of All Time

We'll admit to being subjective here, and maybe some of you will think we're wrong; but after taking a close look at the world of game shows, we've come to some conclusions and are willing to go out on a limb. Granted, even the best minds in television can make a mistake, and one man's champagne is another's Draino. Cheap excuses and questions of taste aside, the following efforts were just bad, bad, bad. These 19 shows were so awful that they don't even deserve to be put in order.

As a matter of fact, we'll space them so you can put them in order yourself or, better yet, create your own list.

Note that some of these selections might also appear in the Winners section because good or bad is often hard to tell in television. And influence is influence.

The $1.98 Beauty Contest

Syndication   *1978*

This frightening beauty pageant parody from the ever-fertile mind of Chuck Barris makes THE GONG SHOW look like a candidate for the Good-Taste Hall of Fame. Ugly people, some with actual defects, and women with extreme conditions of one kind or another, competed for almost nothing and were judged by the likes of Rex Reed and Dr. Joyce "how the mighty have fallen" Brothers. It proved that host Rip Taylor must have really needed a job.

Sense and Nonsense

NBC   *1953*

A lot of time and effort goes into the creation of a game show, the problem is a lot of it is wasted. Maybe the creators of this one needed to spend a little time out of the institution, or maybe they were just desperate. SENSE AND NONSENSE, a show in which contestants were actually expected to recognize things by their smell, sound, taste, etc., wins the "I'll Watch Anything, Mabel" award for commitment to lethargy and the decline of western civilization. Even the producers couldn't come up with a reason why the Bob Kennedy hosted effort didn't stink the place up. The execs at the network soon agreed.

Showdown

NBC   *1966*

Think of those responsible for creating the things we watch on television as feeders at a zoo that sometimes runs out of meat. The hungry monster demands to be fed and so the keepers are often forced to improvise a meal. How else can we imagine anyone coming up with the idea for a game show in which the penalty for a wrong answer was that the chair the contestant was sitting in would break away, spilling the chump on the floor. Joe Pyne, one of the pioneers of the nasty and provocative interview, was the host.

Finders Keepers

NBC   1951
DUMONT   1954

To be contestants in this zany effort people had to be willing to vacant their own personal homes and let strangers from the network hide a prize while the crew set up all the equipment necessary for a remote broadcast (which in those days was considerable). Then, while all America watched and host Fred Robbins monitored their progress, the contestants got to tear their homes apart looking for the prize. We will admit that remotes were a big deal in the early days of television, but we fought a war with the British for the right to keep strangers out of our houses—even if they wanted to hide stuff.

Balance Your Budget

CBS   1953

If this show aired today, those responsible would risk being run out of town on a rail. A "little woman" came on the program and told Bert Parks why she couldn't handle the family finances. Then she got a chance to pull herself out of the red with a simple Q&A.

With This Ring

DUMONT   *1951*

A forerunner of humiliating couples shows to come, this effort allowed a boy and girl, recently engaged, to run a gauntlet of marriage counselors and therapists who made some educated guesses about whether or not the pair would survive in the marriage jungle. The winning couple got a free honeymoon. The losers got neuroses and perhaps sought therapy from the panelists.

Dream House

ABC   *1968*

Amazingly, this show was thought up by the man responsible for the classy THE G.E. COLLEGE BOWL, Don Reid. Maybe his cousin, (and host) Mike Darrow needed a job. Young married couples, desperate for new digs, could win furniture, room by room; or, if they did really well, they could get a trailer house "put anywhere in the USA."

Sandblast

MTV   *1994*

Best described as AMERICAN GLADIATORS on an Orlando inlet, the show, which is still on the air, features lots of sex, sun, and skimpy swimsuits. Hard bodies—displaying as many body parts as cable will allow—compete in odd contests of strength and skills developed by the unemployed. The show is hosted by a team of terminally hip idiots who are better left unidentified. It may be that this special kind of outdoor weirdness happens only in Florida because this show reminds us of another awful show, TREASURE ISLE, that we'll get to later.

The Comeback Story

ABC   *1953*

It makes sense that George Jessel would take the reins of a show whose aim was to give a second chance to celebs whose careers had hit bottom. But that Arlene Francis, one of the all-time game show icons, would take it over is chilling. After the has-beens performed their sad and sometimes embarrassing acts, the viewing audience judged their efforts with the dreaded applause meter. THE COMEBACK STORY lasted less than five months.

Personals

NBC   *1991*

Late night was the right time for what is possibly the bottom of the game show barrel. Maybe after midnight wasn't late enough for this sleazy clone of THE DATING GAME in which inane guys out of Miller Lite commercials tried to get dates with beach-bunny types after watching video clips or ads. Michael Berger was at the helm of a ship that sank to new depths but didn't drown.

Pet loving guests prepare to explore their compatibility in the final round of PERSONALS.

Haggis Baggis

NBC   *1958*

You have to live in an ivory tower inhabited only by creatives and other toadies who are paid to agree with you to think that HAGGIS BAGGIS is a good title for anything except a landfill boutique somewhere in Jersey. Poor Jack Linkletter.

Make Me Laugh

ABC   *1958*
Syndicated   *1979*

The amazing thing is that somebody thought that a show which ran for two months in 1958 was worth syndicating in 1979. People who spend too much time in padded network rooms just don't learn. Three borscht-belt comics, Sid Gould, Buddy Lester, and Henny Youngman, confronted contestants and tried to make them laugh. The contestants who didn't won a prize. The show was hosted by Robert Q. Lewis, who should have known better.

Let's See

ABC   *1955*

The award for the most blatant self-promotion on a game show goes to this effort sponsored by the Atlantic City Chamber of Commerce. Aging pioneer-host John Reed King asked contestants stupid questions about the wonderful things they had seen in Atlantic City. Sense the desperation, feel the pity. The show lasted a month and perhaps is the mother of all infomercials.

100 Grand

ABC   *1963*

A huge publicity campaign ushered in this attempt to bring trust, honesty, and entertainment back to big-prize game shows and ratings back to the networks after the scandals of the late 50s. The show pitted amateurs against experts in a contest of intelligence. The amateurs sat in high-tech isolation booths complete with encyclopedias from which were gathered really obscure information. Impossible questions were passed to the other team by beautiful assistants. If this sounds hard, it was. The "experts" missed every question in the first round. Nobody won, so it was also really boring. Jack Clark only had to host it twice before it sank beneath its own weight and made everyone nostalgic for old Charles Van Doren and the gang at TWENTY–ONE.

E.S.P.

ABC   *1958*

Not even celebrity, actor, and professional scary guy Vincent Price could stem the overwhelming tide of negative public opinion toward this silly attempt at testing how successfully people could use their powers of extrasensory perception. After only three airings in the dead of summer 1958 they tried to make it into a drama and failed.

Legends Of The Hidden Temple

Nickelodeon   *1994*

It's hard to knock a bunch of kids dressed up in helmets, pads, and brightly colored T-shirts running around in a politically correct Indiana Jones type environment searching for treasure, but we'll do it anyway. Some things may be fun to actually do but certainly not to watch. Maybe we're just too old to be enthralled by giant stone faces made out of cheap canvas and sounding like James Earl Jones giving clues about where to find trinkets hidden in a cheap imitation of the Temple of Doom.

Contestants at the starting line for SUPERMARKET SWEEP. Host Bill Malone prepares to give some eager shoppers the go.

Supermarket Sweep

ABC   *1965*

When host Bill Malone said "Go", three housewives, or the occasional male of the species, complete with shopping carts and a friend, were set loose in a supermarket. Rushing against the time limit, the couple who managed to bag the highest dollar amount before the buzzer buzzed was the winner. They got to go again. They also got to keep what they took. The big winner in the 60s version was a Mrs. Harold Rathson who was able to harvest 35 turkeys, 22 lawn chairs, and 100 pounds of meat and canned goods in the required amount of time. Life in the fast lane. THE NEW SUPERMARKET SWEEP is curently seen on Lifetime, proving something.

You're In The Picture

CBS   *1961*

This show has the distinction of making a place for itself as a Winner and a Loser. Jackie Gleason was a funny man and he was paid a lot of money to be a funny man. But nobody was ever funny enough to save this turkey. You're In The Picture may have been the only game show to be canceled on the air by its own host.

Contestants had to stick their heads through carnival cutouts and guess what scene was being depicted beneath them while Jackie asked them questions and said funny things. Gleason watched this madness for as long as he could stand it, and when the audience tuned in the next Friday night they saw a bare stage and "The Great One" sitting in an armchair with what looked to be a stiff drink in his hand. "I apologize for insulting your intelligence," he said. "From now on I'll stick to comedy." He did.

"The Great One" tells it like it is. YOU'RE IN THE PICTURE was not
Jackie Gleason's greatest showbiz moment but he was the first to admit it.

Treasure Isle

ABC   *1968*

The winner of the "Why Do I Do This? Because I Can!" award goes to millionaire John D. McArthur, the man whose foundation sponsors the "genius" grants for worthy individuals. John had some unused real estate on the property of his fabulous Palm Beach Hotel, so in the tradition of "If you build it they will come," he created this elaborate tropical setting for a game show and included a grandstand for the studio audience. ABC picked up the ball and TREASURE ISLE was born. What was unfortunate was that people had to play it.

Two couples were furnished with rubber rafts; the husbands had to paddle, blindfolded, across a lagoon while their wives picked up foam pieces of a jigsaw puzzle. When they reached the island, the couple had to solve the puzzle by placing the pieces on a giant easel. Shall we go on? OK, lets.

The puzzle was a stupid riddle, the answer to which floated in a lagoon attached to a buoy. Husbands were steered to the buoy by their wives who stood on the beach with remote controls. Once hubby got the answer, the race was on to ring a big ship's bell hooked up to a fake palm tree on another beach. The winners got the chance to go to yet another island and search for prizes. There never seemed to be much joy in any of this, and even the bubbling host, John Bartholomew Tucker, seemed to have moments of frustration. At least suntans weren't verbotten in '68.

Space for Your Personal Top Ten List of the
Worst Game Shows Ever

1. _____

2. _____

3. _____

4. _____

5. _____

6. _____

7. _____

8. _____

9. _____

10. _____

Robert Strom, a big winner on THE $64,000 CHALLENGE and Art Linkletter compare stock tips for a segment on PEOPLE ARE FUNNY.

Quiz 3: A Little Game Show Backstage Trivia

Everyone But The Contestants: A Quiz In Three Parts

Consider that we've been playing games over the airwaves for over 70 years, and for each one of those 70 years somebody somewhere has been collecting and saving information. It's not surprising that there's a lot of trivia out there just waiting to pop out, befuddle, and confuse the most ardent game show fan. We've done our best to put together some tough, but answerable, questions. The dyed-in-the-wool couch potato can take heart because the answers are on pages 276 though 278.

And away we go!

Leo, You're Outta Here ...

When baseball manager Leo Durocher had a hard time recognizing the tune "Sympathy" on NAME THAT TUNE he was prompted with the clue: "It's something an umpire needs beginning with's.'" His response? "A seeing-eye dog."

A Little Game Show Backstage Trivia: Part One

1. What celebrity hosted quiz shows under two different names?

2. Rudolph Wanderone, Jr., hosted a show called CELEBRITY BILLIARDS but did not use his given name. Who was Rudy when he was on camera?

3. Professional tennis player Bobby Riggs, who hosted CELEBRITY TENNIS, put on a dress to play who on national television in the mid-70s?

4. Name three other professional athletes who have worked the microphone as hosts?

5. Dick Butkus worked a show called STAR GAMES, but he was a star in his own right. What was his title on the show and what was Dick's other claim to fame?

6. Ralph Edwards hosted TRUTH OR CONSEQUENCES but was best known as host for what phenomenally successful television show of the 1950s?

7. Wally Cox of THE HOLLYWOOD SQUARES grew up in the same small Nebraska town and was best friends with one of the most famous actors of all time. Name him.

8. What celebrity game show host actually canceled his own show on the air?

9. Name the JEOPARDY! world champion who went on to be a producer and game show developer. Hint: He produced THE NEW PRICE IS RIGHT.

(answers on page 276)

A Little Game Show Backstage Trivia: Part Two

1. One of the stars of *Rebel Without A Cause* tested stunts for over a year on BEAT THE CLOCK. Who was he? (Hint: Elvis thought he was the greatest actor in the world.)

2. Name five famous newscasters who also hosted game shows and one of the shows each did.

3. One of America's most famous songwriters was a regular on MUSICAL CHAIRS. Who was he?

4. Regis Philbin is very well known these days for his partnership with Kathy Lee Gifford on their successful morning talk show, *Live With Regis and Kathy Lee*. But Regis also toiled in the game show vineyards. Name the show he hosted and the show he assisted on.

5. She went on to write some pretty steamy novels, but in the beginning she did a stint as hostess on a show called YOUR SURPRISE STORE. Who is she?

6. These guys may be the only brothers to host game shows using the same last name. Who are they?

7. Two ventriloquists have hosted game shows. Who are they and what were the shows?

8. The person responsible for the voices of Bugs Bunny, Elmer Fudd, and many more of our cartoon favorites was also a regular panelist on MUSICAL CHAIRS. Name Him.

9. Merv Griffin began his career as a singer. Name three of his former employers.

(answers on page 277)

The Price for Success on The $64,000 Question in 1955

At the various stages of the show, how much did a contestant have left after taxes?

Assuming a spouse and two children, a gross annual income of $5,000 and the standard 10% tax deduction, here's how much was really won:

Prize	After Taxes
$ 1,000	$ 820
2,000	1,640
4,000	3,246
8,000	6,324
16,000	11,956
32,000	21,220
64,000	34,460

A Little Game Show Backstage Trivia: Part Three

1. Can you name two famous talk show hosts who also did game shows?

2. A panelist on QUIZZING THE NEWS, he created syndicated comic strip Steve Canyon. Who was he?

3. As manager of the Detroit Tigers he was noted for the size of his mouth, so it was a natural career step for the "Lip" to become host of JACKPOT BOWLING. What's his name?

4. Former Miss America, CBS sportscaster, panelist on I'VE GOT A SECRET. Who is she?

5. As announcer extraodinaire, Johnny Olson's voice was heard on 24 shows including THE PRICE IS RIGHT, WHAT'S MY LINE?, I'VE GOT A SECRET, and more; but he made it in front of the camera as host only once. What was the show?

6. One long-running panel show has the distinction of sharing two ex-athletes as hosts. One played baseball and the other was a multiple Super Bowl winner. Who are the jocks and what was the show?

7. Name the only game show panelist to be a victim of the McCarthy hearings of the 1950s.

8. Two famous comics tried to imitate Groucho's success with reissues of YOU BET YOUR LIFE. Who were they?

9. Gil Fates was the host of HOLD IT PLEASE, CBS's early home-phone quiz show in 1949. He went on to produce three big-time game shows. What were they?

(answers on page 278)

An Inside Look at How JEOPARDY! Was Born

"Creating a game isn't like conceiving a drama when you say, 'let's do something about a transit cop' or 'let's do something about a woman private eye who does karate.' In drama you can reach out and pick up a start-off notion. In games you begin with a blank page. It's almost like trying to create a new sport. Think of a new sport. Think of how few new sports really come along." —Producer Mark Goodson

Some people seem to have obsessive genetic inclinations that drive them to create games. We can imagine Mr. Goodson and Mr. Todman as youngsters in the backyard saying things like "OK, Randy let's turn the orange crate into the podium and you be the host. OK? And the panel is gonna sit by the wall, and we're gonna ask the questions; and if you're wrong, you gotta do what we say. OK?"

They couldn't help themselves then, and they can't help themselves now. Grown men have interrupted well-deserved vacations in exotic places to rush back to New York and pitch an idea for a big-money quiz show (THE $64,000 QUESTION) to the network. They sit in expensive restaurants and try to guess the occupations of the people sitting around them (WHAT'S MY LINE?). They have dreams of flashing lights and moving squares (PRESS YOUR LUCK) and of people racing to ring bells when they recognize a song (NAME THAT TUNE).

Sometimes, like obsessive gamester Merv Griffin, they just realize that the ANSWER is really the question. That's what hit Merv and his wife like a bolt of thunder on a red-eye flight from Los Angeles to New York back in 1962. It was out of that flash of inspiration that one of the most original ideas for a quiz show was born. Eventually it would be called JEOPARDY!.

Merv had a deal to develop game shows for NBC. If you think about it, this was a tough assignment. The scandals of the 50s were barely out of memory and the networks were nervous about anything that could possibly be perceived as fixed. On the other hand, the big-money shows like "QUESTION" and "TWENTY-ONE" were the ones that blew the ratings off the charts. Large prizes for contestants equaled large revenues for the network. Merv had a mission but no ideas until his wife suggested a little twist, the gist of which was give the contestants the answers and let them come up with the questions.

Griffin hit the tarmac running. He rushed to the office and started getting the idea on its feet. He decided to break the answers into gen-

---

What Is 350,750?

The JEOPARDY! team produces an average of 230 shows per year and they've been doing it for close to 25 years. Each show contains 61 "answers" that are used in the "Jeopardy!," "Double Jeopardy!," and "Final Jeopardy!" rounds. The calculator tells us that's 14,030 answers a year. So the question is... How many answers have been used on JEOPARDY! since the show began?

---

eral categories like literature, music, and history, put them on a board in columns, and give them dollar values. Griffin and his staff called the game WHAT'S THE QUESTION? and sent the concept to a scenic house to build a mock-up of the game board so they could make a live presentation to NBC execs.

NBC was interested enough to give them development money. Merv took the game home, literally. He conned friends and neighbors over to his apartment and tried out variations and ideas. Out of these living-room production meetings came the rounds of play with names like Jeopardy!, Double Jeopardy! and Final Jeopardy!. WHAT'S THE QUESTION? became JEOPARDY! when a network exec appraised the progress and told Merv he liked what he was seeing but felt the show needed more jeopardies.

After months of demanding and often difficult work, JEOPARDY! was ready for another run-through at the network. In the NBC board room

---

Let The Games Begin!

The world was waiting with bated breath. The press room in Atlanta was jammed with reporters from all over the world. The announcement finally came.

Yes, it was true.

In February of 1995, JEOPARDY! and WHEEL OF FORTUNE were named the official game shows of the 1996 Summer Olympics. Alex, Pat, and Vanna are going for the gold!

Merv rigged an easel with envelopes containing answer cards representing the categories. The head of NBC at the time, a fellow named Mort Werner, was designated the member of the studio audience. He watched as the presentation unfolded. As the rounds progressed he became more and more frustrated and, when it was over, stated emphatically that the game was too hard. A young executive assistant dared to disagree. He argued that network should buy the show. Finally Mort agreed but made it clear that if the show was a flop, a particular assistant's head would roll. The assistant's name? Grant Tinker, who went on to become one of the most successful television producers of all time. There were bumps along the way, but JEOPARDY! aired in 1963 with master quizmaster Art Fleming, and it has been a fixture in homes here and abroad ever since. (Alex Trebek is now the host.)

Without Grant's instinct for what could succeed on network television, JEOPARDY!—one of the most successful game shows of all time—could have ended as nothing more than another unsuccessful pitch and some crumpled paper in Merv's trash can. By the way, Merv even wrote the JEOPARDY! theme song. Now that's hands on.

> *"I'm from the Goodson-Todman school of games. If you can't explain it in one sentence, it won't work."*
> —*Merv Griffin*

What's She Going To Do?

Within four weeks of its premier on June 7, 1955 THE $64,000 QUESTION was the nation's #1 show with a whopping 23.1 in the Trendex lineup. But that was only the beginning; week five logged in at 43. This somehow (nobody understood Trendex any better than Neilson when it came to ratings) translated into the fact that 79.4% of the available television sets in the country were tuned in to find out if Mrs. Catherine Kreitzer would stop at $32,000 or go for $64,000. Millions watched as Mrs. Kreitzer took the money and ran.

JUST THE FACTS, MA'AM...

The Game Shows and the Networks, Syndicators, and Cable Companies

Game shows are like people, they need a roof over their heads to survive and flourish. Game shows are also like people in that they move around, get kicked out, or just retire after a busy and productive life. But like we said in the beginning, everybody's got to have a place to hang his hat. Following are the places where the quiz shows live and work.

What The Heck Is A Network?

Everyone knows the names of the major television networks, but how many of us actually know what television networks are.

The majors, ABC, CBS, and NBC, are chains of stations throughout the country connected by satellite for efficient distribution of programming and advertising. The programming is broadcast free to consumers; all they need is an antenna and the patience to watch the average ten minutes of commercials that are part of each broadcasting hour. Execs actually refer to programming as the air space between commercials.

Game shows were perfect material for networks from the very beginning. At their best they are exciting and inexpensive, relative to other kinds of shows; and at their worst they are awful and inexpensive, relative to the same thing.

Today, each of the major original networks has about 200 stations or affiliates that pay for programming provided to them by the network. It's basic economic theory: since a group has more resources and power than an individual, the group will tend to dominate the market. Early broadcasting execs quickly recognized the enormous potential of television and began immediately to band stations together in order to control the market and the advertising revenues. The men in charge were tough, competitive, and successful; and they convinced themselves that they were invulnerable.

The networks grew fat, lazy, and rich and the system worked like a charm until advances in technology made possible alternatives—such as cable, UHF, and upstart networks such as FOX, UNIVERSAL, and PARAMOUNT. Suddenly, there were alternatives for the viewing audience, and the affiliates, which had been forced to take pretty much what the networks were serving up, started to feel the pinch as they lost advertising revenues to the new kids on the block.

There's no doubt that after so many years on top of the heap the networks are feeling the strain of competition and only time will tell which ones are going to be the big dogs in 2001.

What The Heck Is Syndication?

Syndication evolved as a means for local and independent stations (those not affiliated with a network) to compete with the more powerful and established networks for programming and audience. For many years syndicating companies developed low-cost and relatively low-tech programming to fill holes in the late afternoon and early evening time slots, knowing that most of the viewers would switch to the networks for prime-time shows.

When the networks began to concentrate on soaps and talk shows for daytime programming, game show producers had to search for new markets and they found them in syndication.

The low production costs of game shows made them ideal fare for independent stations and the 60s and 70s saw some classic and many questionable contests enter and exit the airwaves. Ironically, the market for mid-level entries has been crippled by the advent of popular and profitable syndicated efforts with high production values, such as *Star Trek: The Next Generation* and the phenomenal success of WHEEL OF FORTUNE and JEOPARDY! which have effectively tied up the early evening time slots on most independent stations. The rise of cable television, along with the emergence of FOX and others, has further eroded the market for syndicating companies as well.

The syndicators and producers who create and market game shows, however, are survivors and know that the market and public taste swing back and forth over time. The cable networks have begun to rerun the classic game shows and develop new entries of their own.

What the heck is Cable?

There was a time in the 60s and early 70s that most people considered cable television (assuming they knew what it was) just a fancy antenna system that ran underground, offered a few more channels, and made reception better in large cities and rural areas. And anyway; it had a downside: the cable company sent you a bill every month.

Today, we're so used to the notion of the little red-eyed box that sits on our home entertainment centers and brings us the world that we forget generations of Americans grew up with the idea that television was free—like their country. There was a lot of resistance to cable especially in the larger cities where viewers had a multitude of stations available just by shifting the rabbit ears.

But there were visionaries who believed that the future was now, and eventually, the venture capitalists and the true believers got together. They figured out that if they offered premium programming such as first-run movies, live concerts, and sporting events without commercial interruptions they might have a place in the market. (That's right, early cable prided itself on no commercial interruptions. How times have changed.) They banked on the idea that future success depended on national cable networks broadcast by satellite and distributed by local cable companies. They were right as rain.

HBO popped out of the box in 1975 and the world changed forever. Today there are more cable networks and channels available than most people have to the ability to remember, and the future promises literally hundreds of viewing options. The Game Show Channel is finally a reality. Hosted by Peter Tomarken, 24 hours of fun and games are available on direct dish and eventually will undoubtedly find a home on cable.

There's no doubt that cable is here to stay. What started in the 40s as a funky little service industry whose major aim was to get rid of the snow and bring in Denver, clear as a bell, has become a giant force in the entertainment and information industry.

I don't care what the auditor said, it was a business lunch, and I want the deduction.

Goodson and Todman often lunched with New York DJ, Bob Bach, who was fascinated with guessing people's occupations. They would place bets on what people around them did for a living and then ask those people to find out. One day it occurred to them that they might have a game show on their hands. CBS agreed and that's how WHAT'S MY LINE? was born. Since it was sort of his idea, Bach came along as an associate producer. We don't know who paid for lunch.

THE END OF INNOCENCE: RIGGING THE GAME SHOWS

Behind The Scandal at TWENTY-ONE

Television is, and has always been, in the business of making money and money in television is made by asking sponsors to pay for the right to advertise their products on shows. The more popular the show, the more it costs to buy advertising time. Hence, the more profits for the network. Producers are expected to develop and maintain hit shows to keep the advertising rates high. If not, the execs will find somebody else who can. It's a tough business, and one that crushes the weak to dust on a daily basis.

Successful producers can smell trends and develop shows that make the most of them. Such was the case with Louis G. Cowan, who felt that the time was right in 1955 for a game show that would celebrate intellect and reward it with almost unimaginable sums of money. Referring to the old radio quiz show TAKE IT OR LEAVE IT, he said that, "the $64 wasn't enough to make news" in 1955 but "$64,000 gets into the realm of the impossible."

THE $64,000 QUESTION premiered on June 7, 1955, and took the viewing public by storm. It became the most popular show on television, knocking even the beloved *I Love Lucy* off the block. The show had it all: a charming host in Hal March, contestants who were recognizable as regular Joes with big minds, and the enticing possibility of reaping a nest-egg that could set winners up for life. Participants could even get a Cadillac as a consolation prize if they blew it.

The contestants were making money, the networks were making money, Revlon (the show's sponsor) was raking it in. The show was a natural, a gold mine, and it set the competition scurrying to find something to put up against it.

Enter Dan Enright and NBC staff-producer Bob Noah, who sat down and devised a concept that had the chance of blowing "QUESTION" out of the water. Based on the card game Blackjack, "TWENTY-ONE" pulled out all the stops. There was more of everything: two contestants, two isolation booths with built-in heaters to help the contestants sweat it out, and the possibility of winning an unlimited amount of money for those who were cool under pressure and very smart. Host Jack Barry announced the category and the contestant decided how many points, from 1 to 11, to bet on whether or not they could answer a question. The first to reach 21 was the winner and could keep coming back until he quit or lost it all. The problem was, the show didn't have any spark, the contestants were eggheads. There was no pizzazz. The sponsor was unhappy. "Fix it," they said. And Enright did.

He approached the show as if it were live theater. He looked for attractive and interesting people and he coached them in how to play for maximum tension and effect. He taught them how to pass from one question to the next to give the impression that the struggle to remember was intense. And he began to feed them the answers. The first contestant to discover that the questions he answered in the coaching session were the ones used on the show refused to continue, but when Enright discovered an ex-GI living in Queens named Herb Stempel, he got the contestant of his dreams.

Stempel cooperated immediately and discovered a natural gift for acting confused and uncertain even though he knew the answer. The viewers seemed to like him. The show was improving, but the pressure was on because TWENTY-ONE was still second cousin to QUESTION and the recent $64,000 CHALLENGE. Though eager and willing, Stempel didn't exude the kind of sensibility that made for gangbuster ratings in middle America. Enright had guessed wrong and was paying the price. Then he met Charles Van Doren.

Handsome and articulate, Van Doren was a producer's dream. Son of a famous and respected scholar and member of a family that lived and breathed intellect and charm, Charles was eking out a living as an associate professor at Columbia until he decided what to do with his life. He decided he wanted to be on a game show. He tried out for TIC TAC DOUGH, another Enright production, but was instantly recognized as a candidate for TWENTY-ONE. The team approached Van Doren and outlined what they wanted him to do. Stempel had to go and Charles was the man to unseat him. Van Doren initially resisted, but the team convinced him with the argument that his presence on the show would elevate the masses and lead them to a renewed respect for learning and intellect. So Charles got on board. Now to deal with Stempel.

Herb did not take kindly to being cut out of the deal. He was enjoying the fame and the money; so when they asked him to take a dive, he was shocked and angry. The thing that irritated him the most was that the question he was supposed to miss was something he knew without being told. *Marty* was his favorite movie, he knew darn well it had won the Academy Award in 1955. Tanking on any other question maybe, but that one? Herbie took the fall, but he didn't want to. It would become the straw that broke the camel's back.

In the meantime, Van Doren proved to be what everyone was looking for. He was dubbed the "Wizard of Quiz." His face was on every magazine cover. He was a tonic for America. His success made Enright a genius. The show exploded. Everybody was doing great, except Herb, who was looking around for somebody to tell how he had been shafted. Probably Enright underestimated the depth of Stempel's anger and his need for revenge. If he had realized, he might have tried to deal with it. But he didn't; and, by hanging Stempel out to dry, he sowed the seeds of his own destruction.

Van Doren lived with the pressure as long as he could and finally gave over the reins to a Ms. Vivenne Nearing when he couldn't come up with the name of the king of Belgium. He left TWENTY-ONE a folk hero with winnings of $129,000 and a brand new job on the *Today* show at $50,000 per. Things looked bright. If he'd been looking up instead of far into the rosy future, he would have seen that the hammer was about to fall.

Stempel was seeking a willing listener, but finding one wasn't as easy as he thought. In the beginning nobody wanted to know. He contacted all the major dailies in New York to no avail. Stempel couldn't give it away. In fact, if it hadn't been for a fellow named Edward

Hilgemeier and a silly little show named DOTTO, Stempel's story probably would have been just another tale of sour grapes echoing out of the neighborhood bars deep in the borough of Queens.

Here's how it happened. Alternate contestant Hilgemeier was backstage waiting for what he hoped would be his big chance. He felt he deserved a shot on DOTTO, which at the time, was one of the most popular game shows on the air. Contestants answered questions which allowed them to connect dots to reveal a drawing of a celebrity. It wasn't big money, but it was fun and was pulling in strong ratings on both its daytime and evening slots. Instead of twiddling his thumbs backstage, Hilgemeier started leafing through a notebook belonging to Marie Winn, a previous contestant and DOTTO winner. To his surprise he discovered that the notebook contained answers to questions she had been asked on the show. He brought it to the attention of the contestant Marie had beaten and when they confronted the producers, they were offered a payoff, which they accepted. So far so good, until Ed, who seems to have had a tendency to be a little nosy, found out that he had gotten less money than his partner. He contacted the Attorney General's office in Manhattan, who notified the FCC, who called the sponsor, Colgate, who canceled the show the next day (August 15, 1958).

About a week later all the papers were suddenly interested in what Herb had to say, and his personal story broke on August 28, 1958. The watchwords at NBC were deny, deny, deny. Enright, Van Doren, and everyone else said it was the ravings of a bitter and crazed loser out to take revenge. But the cat was out of the bag, and there was no putting it back. Ratings plummeted and sponsors fled in droves. A grand jury met in New York but never released its findings. The president of the United States added some fuel to the fire by insisting that the public would not rest until the mess was cleaned up. Up on Capitol Hill Rep. Oren Harris got his subcommittee investigation rolling. Herb took the train to Washington and talked a blue streak; but, just as was the case on TWENTY-ONE, his ratings weren't high enough. Everybody wanted to talk to Charlie, who did his best to avoid the issue, until a congressional subpoena found its way to his home in New York. He went to Washington on November 2, 1958, and spilled the beans. He lost respect, he lost his jobs at Columbia and at NBC, but at least he told the truth. It was the end of an era; it was the end of innocence. Congress passed legislation making it illegal to fix game shows.

The question is, what really happened? What's the bottom line? Well, the bottom line on all this is a little strange. In a way Enright had been right, rigging had made for electric and exciting television viewing. Consider a perspiring Van Doren, alone in the isolation booth, struggling to answer a difficult question with the game and a fortune at stake. Could he do it? America was on the edge of its collective chair and maybe, if the truth had not come out, his success would have furthered the cause of education and the love of knowledge that Enright had enticed him with some months before. It may have been great theater, but it was empty at the center because it was all a fake.

In the end a lot of people suffered. Careers went down the tubes, reputations were destroyed. A producer named Freedman spent two years in jail for perjury. In all, 23 contestants on various game shows admitted guilt to one degree or other. Enright and Noah admitted the show was rigged. They admitted that all their shows were rigged. They said it was standard television practice and was about showmanship and show business and exciting viewing. It wasn't really fraud. "Who really got hurt?" they asked. The public had a great time; the contestants made some money as did the sponsors and the networks. OK, Enright and Noah made a little themselves. After all the disclaimers, Noah, Enright, and the rest all said they were sorry and that they shouldn't have misled the viewing public and promised not to do it again.

Ironically, most of the people involved came out of it just fine. After a few years on the outs Enright and Barry combined to produce THE JOKER's WILD and from that created a game show business that was far more successful than anything they had done before. Van Doren survived to work for Encyclopedia Britannica and has written several children's books. Stempel went into the woodwork somewhere.

The problem is we expect our heroes to be honest and quizzes aren't quizzes if we already know the answers. The lie was in the breaking of faith between Charlie and all the people out there who wanted and needed to believe in him.

The Real Nitty-Gritty:

Actual Words from the Congressional Committee

Hearings before a Subcommittee of the Committee on Interstate and Foreign Commerce, House of Representatives, Eighty-Sixth Congress, First Session, October 6, 7, 8, 9 , 10 and 12 (part one), *November 2, 3, 4, 5, and 6, 1959* (part two), United States Government Printing Office 1960.

Ladies and gentlemen...

Welcome to the old House Office Building in beautiful downtown Washington D.C., I'm your host, the Hon. Oren Harris, Representative for the great state of Washington, and it's time tooo teessstify! First let's hear from Mr. Charles Van Doren of New York City!

Testimony of Charles Van Doren, Monday, November 2, 1959

I would give almost anything I have to reverse the course of my life in the last three years. I cannot take back one word or action; the past does not change for anyone. But at least I can learn from the past.

I have learned a lot in those three years, especially in the last three weeks. I've learned a lot about life. I've learned a lot about myself, and about the responsibilities any man has to his fellow men. I've learned a lot about good and evil. They are not always what they appear to be. I was involved, deeply involved, in a deception. The fact that I, too, was very much deceived cannot keep me from being the principal victim of that deception, because I was its principal symbol.

I have a long way to go. I have deceived my friends, and I had millions of them.

Before my first appearance on TWENTY–ONE I was asked by [Albert] Friedman [the producer of TIC TAC DOUGH] to come to his apartment. He took me into his bedroom where we could talk alone. He told me that Herbert Stempel, the current champion, was an unbeatable contestant because he knew too much. He said that Stempel was unpopular and was defeating opponents right and left to the detriment of the program. He asked me if, as a favor to him, I would agree to make an arrangement whereby I would tie Stempel and thus increase the entertainment value of the program.

I asked him to let me go on the program honestly, without receiving help. He said that was impossible. He told me that I would not have a chance to defeat Stempel because he was too knowledgeable. He also told me that the show was merely entertainment and that giving help to quiz contestants was a common practice and merely a part of show business. This, of course, was not true, but perhaps I wanted to believe him. He also stressed the fact that by appearing on a nationally televised program I would be doing a great service to the intellectual life, to teachers and to education in general, by increasing public respect for the work of the mind through my performances. In fact, I think I have done a disservice to all of them. I deeply regret this, since I believe nothing is of more vital importance to our civilization than education. Whenever I hesitated or expressed uneasiness at the course events were taking during my time on the program, the same sort of discussion ensued, and, foolishly and wrongly, I persuaded myself that it was all true. Freedman guaranteed me $1,000 if I would appear for one night.

I met him next at his office, where he explained how the program would be controlled. He told me the questions I was to be asked, and then asked if I could answer them. Many of them I could. But he was dissatisfied with my answers. They were not "entertaining" enough. He instructed me how to answer the questions: to pause before certain of the answers, to skip certain parts and return to them, to hesitate and build up suspense, and so forth....

I was deeply troubled by the arrangement. As time went on, the show ballooned beyond my wildest expectations. I had supposed I would win a few thousand dollars and be known to a small television audience. But from an unknown college instructor I became a celebrity. I received thousands of letters and dozens of requests to make speeches, appear in movies, and so forth. To a certain extent this went to my head. I was almost able to convince myself that it did not matter what I was doing because it was having such a good effect on the national attitude toward teachers, education, and the intellectual life. At the same time I was winning more money than I had ever had or even dreamed of having. I was able to convince myself that I could make up for it after it was over. Again, I do not wish to emphasize my mental and moral struggles. Yet the public renown also made me terribly uncomfortable.

I was, of course, very foolish. I was incredibly naive.

Boy, that was something. How about you, Xavier? Anything to say for yourself?

Testimony of Xavier Cugat, Bandleader
Tuesday, November 3, 1959

As it turned out, the studying was not necessary. A day or so before the first program went on the air, a member of the producer's staff came to my apartment. When he arrived, we sat down and he asked me a series of questions. I knew the answers to some of those questions, but I didn't know the answers to others. When I didn't know the answers, he gave me the answers and the questions.

I know that as an entertainer I am called upon all the time to make-believe, to help make a good show. I suppose the producers of THE $64,000 CHALLENGE also wanted to make a better show, and so they made believe, too. If there was too much make-believe, I wish you could do something about it without giving entertainment too much of a black eye.

Well, I can see where you're coming from Mr. Cugat. Now surely, Mr. Revson, you must have been aware of something?

Testimony of Charles Revson,
president of the Revlon Co.
Wednesday, November 4, 1959

Sure, I was the sponsor, but I was just like the rest of the millions of Americans who had been caught up in the drama of this program.

If I had known that these shows were fixed, crooked, rigged, do you think for one minute that I would have watched or bothered this way? And yet I heard for the first time last week, and you heard the testimony yesterday, that they were rigging the show right from the start with some of the earliest contestants. This was a time when THE $64,000 QUESTION was at its peak, when its ratings were at their highest. I was absolutely flabbergasted.

So were we. Maybe it's time to get the producer's side of the story. Mr Enright, Mr. Lishman would like to ask you a few questions.

Testimony of Daniel Enright, producer of TWENTY–ONE Tuesday, October 6, 1959

Excerpted from Mr. Enright's examination by Robert W. Lishman, counsel to the subcommittee.

> MR. LISHMAN: Did you furnish questions and answers in advance to Mr. [Herbert] Stempel?
>
> MR. ENRIGHT: I did.
>
> MR. LISHMAN: Did you furnish questions and answers in advance to Mr. [Richard] Jackman.
>
> MR. ENRIGHT: I did.
>
> MR. LISHMAN: Did you furnish questions and answers in advance to other contestants?
>
> MR. ENRIGHT: One or two more, to the best of my recollection.
>
> MR. LISHMAN: Did you coach them on how to act when they appeared on the program?
>
> MR. ENRIGHT: I did.

QUIZ 4:
THE SCANDALS

If I Already Knew the Answer,
Wouldn't It Be Easier to Play the Game?

Charles Van Doren after losing
to Vivenne Nearing on TWENTY-ONE.

136

Scandals
Quiz

1. What was the first show to be involved in the quiz scandals? Who was the host?

2. Who was Edward Hilgemeier, Jr., and what was the discovery he made that rocked an industry?

3. Someone who became a regular panelist on the GONG SHOW made her television debut as a big winner on The $64,000 Question. Who was she?

4. Name the show that was called in to replace TWENTY-ONE in the aftermath of the rigging scandal? It went on to become a major game show success.

5. Who was the congressman in charge of investigating allegations of rigging in the game show industry?

6. What was the official title of the 1,156 pages of testimony the Government Printing office saved for posterity?

7. Who was the first winner on THE $64,000 QUESTION?

8. Who was the first contestant to actually win $64,000?

9. Who was the sponsor for THE $64,000 QUESTION and what was the product that was pitched?

10. Dan Enright, one of the show's creators, had a trick for making the contestants on TWENTY-ONE look like they were working hard even though they already knew the answers. What was it?

(answers on page 278)

There Must Have Been
A Lot to Say.

The testimony before the House Committee that investigated the game show scandals filled two volumes and was 1,156 pages long. Volume 1 was 622 pages in length and Volume 2 was, of course, 534.

11. The first contestant Enright approached to go along with rigging the show refused. Who was he?

12. Who was the first to accept?

13. How much did Stempel win on TWENTY-ONE before he got the ax?

14. What was Charles Van Doren's nickname?

15. Which national magazine broke stories of rigging on the big-money game shows, as early as 1957?

16. What newspapers did Stempel call to leak his story?

17. An actress, whose most recent television series is *Amazing Grace*, was called to testify before the committee on the scandals. Who is she?

18. What was CBS's executive response to the leaking of the TWENTY-ONE scandal?

19. What was Charles Van Doren's salary as a teacher before he cashed in on TWENTY-ONE?

20. Jack Barry and Dan Enright made a comeback into the game show world in 1972 with what show?

21. How did Barry and Enright justify giving contestants the answers beforehand?

22. What was the first game show CBS bought after the rigging scandals?

23. A young assistant host on TWENTY-ONE went on to fame and fortune after the scandals. Who was he, and where was he from?

(answers on page 279)

An Inside Look At...

The Ratings Wars:
Survival of the Fittest

We, the viewing audience, watch television to relax and forget the cares of the day. Feet up, lie back, take a break. The networks, on the other hand, never rest. Programmers, producers, and execs get paid big bucks to predict trends and develop shows that will tickle our fancy, stifle the competition, drive the ratings off the charts, and bring home buckets of cash from hungry advertisers. It's win or lose, no middle ground, because we're tough, demanding, and very hard to second guess. Worse, the networks don't really know what we're thinking until Mr. Nielson tells them we've turned off the set or switched the channel. This drives TV producers batty. For every success there are a hundred failures. It's a jungle out there.

The successful show creates a huge problem for the opposition. The other networks don't have any choice but to put their own offerings up against the smash hits and hope the thumping won't hurt too badly. Prime-time slots become bloody battlegrounds where shows drop like flies and careers fizzle. When a TV program catches our imagination, Lord help the competition.

Take a look at a list of the opponents who fell to that ratings juggernaut called THE PRICE IS RIGHT, during it's almost 30-year run.

THE ALL-STAR BLITZ	JEOPARDY!
ALL-STAR SECRETS	Laverne and Shirley
Another World	Love, American Style
Arthur Godfrey Time	The Love Boat
BARGAIN HUNTERS	The Love Report
BATTLESTARS	Loving
Benson	Morning Court
BRUCE FORSYTH'S HOT STREAK	Mr. Belvedere
CELEBRITY SWEEPSTAKES	PASSWORD PLUS
CONCENTRATION	The Real McCoys
David Letterman	Sanford and Son
Dick Van Dyke	SCRABBLE
DOUBLE EXPOSURE	Tennessee Ernie Ford
DOUBLE TALK	The Texan
DREAM HOUSE	Texas
Fame, Fortune and Romance	Three's a Crowd
FAMILY FEUD	Three's Company
The Gale Storm Show	Too Close For Comfort
General Hospital	TRIVIA TRAP
Happy Days	The Verdict Is Yours
HIGH ROLLERS	VIDEO VILLAGE
Hit Man	Webster
THE HOLLYWOOD SQUARES	WHAT'S THIS SONG?
I Love Lucy (reruns)	WHEEL OF FORTUNE
Jane Wyman	WORD FOR WORD

No wonder network execs get migraines!!

MR. CULLEN, THE BUNNIES ARE HERE...

The Playboy Connection

And then there were the game show hostesses who displayed more than the show's prizes...

Playboy magazine picked these four — sometimes before anyone knew their true value:

◆ **Janice Pennington** — MAY 1971.
She prepped for game shows as the lovely assistant to "The Great Martino", Dick Martin's bumbling escape artist on *Rowan and Martin's Laugh-In.* Later she became a hostess on THE PRICE IS RIGHT.

◆ **Suzanne Somers** — FEBRUARY 1980, DECEMBER 1984.
In 1969 she was hostess of THE ANNIVERSARY GAME; later she starred in *Three's Company.*

◆ **Vanna White** — MAY 1987.
Photos taken when she was an aspiring model reveal the WHEEL OF FORTUNE letter turner. This issue was a sellout.

◆ **Dian Parkinson** — DECEMBER 1991.
Readers had been asking for a photo spread since she first appeared on THE PRICE IS RIGHT in 1975. But she was "...shy...kind of a prude."

Here are a few revealing quotes:

"It's harder than it looks... You'd be surprised how many girls couldn't smile. I guess they couldn't warm up to a refrigerator,"
— Dian Parkinson, on her audition

142

"I'm not in such a hurry that I'd play a role I didn't feel was right for me... I'd love to play someone slightly mad. I don't necessarily mean a villainess, just someone kind of flipped out. That would be fascinating and challenging."

—Janice Pennington, *as an aspiring actress*

"We'd spend a fortune to have this sexy star spin our wheel."

—Playboy, *naming Vanna White "Best Game Show Hostess," March 1986*

Aside from the May 1987 photo spread, Vanna has appeared in a number of individual photos:

October 1985	March 1986
July 1986	December 1986
December 1987	December 1988
February 1988	January 1994

A Close Family

Following Dorothy Kilgallen's death in 1965, the WHAT'S MY LINE? team began the painful search for someone to take her place. Daly likened the hunt for a new panelist to the storybook search for Cinderella. "We have to be sure her foot fits the glass slipper. If she doesn't fit into our family, we'll just freeze her out." A Cinderella was never found.

$64,000 Was Chicken Feed

If you're looking to really hit it big on a game show, look at those associated with state lotteries. With names like HOOSIER MILLIONAIRE, ILLINOIS INSTANT RICHES, CASH EXPLOSION, or simply THE BIG MONEY SHOW, there's no doubt what these shows are all about. Getting rich.

It's as true for the states that sponsor these shows as it is for the players. The whole idea of these game shows is to create excitement—and boost the sale of lottery tickets.

The lotteries are winners: Most shows can claim top ratings in their time slots.

And players are winners—big time: Prizes range from $20,000 to $2 million, with most top winners pulling down cash in the $100,000 to $200,000 range.

Drawing on decades of television game shows—Massachusetts, California and Illinois even utilize the expertise of game show pioneers Goodson Productions—the lotteries have come up with rules that are pretty consistent from state to state:

Contestants qualify after recording a winning score on a scratch-off ticket. Then the games rely on flashing lights, bouncing balls, giant pinball machines, numbered doors—and lots of luck. As extensions of lotteries, these games are designed to require no skill at all.

Consider:

◆ In the first nine years after its 1985 premiere, California's BIG SPIN awarded more than $574 million to over 4,100 winners, including

Big Spin host Larry Anderson gets ready to make somebody rich in the
California State Lottery.

286 players who have won $1 million or more.

♦ "Saying so is practically blasphemous, but we even outdraw Indiana University basketball."   —*Hoosier Lottery spokesman Kip Coons*

♦ "If you get the right kind of game show, everybody wants to watch it. Our job is to bring as many eyeballs as we can on a tonnage basis to the set and convert them to lottery players."   — *Jonathan Goodson, head of Goodson Productions and son of founder Mark Goodson*

♦ The Ohio Lottery's CASH EXPLOSION averages 2 million viewers a week. It's the number one program in its time slot in nine markets, including Cincinnati, Cleveland and Columbus.

♦ On THE MONEY GAME SHOW in Wisconsin, even the audience wins. The program takes the total winnings of the five finalists, matches that amount and divides by the total left in the audience—guaranteeing each audience member a minimum of $400.

Here are the states with lottery game shows:

   ♦ CALIFORNIA

   ♦ ILLINOIS

   ♦ INDIANA

   ♦ MASSACHUSETTS

   ♦ MICHIGAN

   ♦ OHIO

   ♦ WISCONSIN

CASH EXPLOSION, The Ohio State Lottery weekly game show, averages 2 million viewers a week, co-hosted by Sharon Bicknell and Paul Tapie.

RIGHT FROM THE SOURCE

A *Bartlett's Quotations* of Game Show One-Liners

═══════════════

"If I had to summarize in one sentence, the major lesson I have learned in life, that sentence would be: 'Sometimes you have to buy a vowel.'"

—Syndicated columnist Dave Barry,
reflecting on his moment on WHEEL OF FORTUNE, May 1995

═══════════════

"It wouldn't be TV at all. It would be theater or movies. I myself don't watch a lot of TV. When I do, it's usually PBS."

—Producer Mark Goodson, when asked whether he would become a game show producer if he could start his career again

"If you haven't heard from us in six months, burn three locks of your hair and try another packager."
    —Heatter-Quigley Productions to hopeful contestants

"Mark and me are very interesting chemistry. We argue constantly. If we both agree, one of us is not doing anything."
    —Bill Todman on his working relationship with Mark Goodson

"It's too hard for me." —Merv Griffin on JEOPARDY!, a show he invented

"There are no brighter stars than those that shine in the day!"
    —Monty Hall, host of LET'S MAKE A DEAL

"Dishing out the truth was OK, it was the consequences I didn't like."

—Jack Bailey, host of TRUTH OR CONSEQUENCES

"If you have lunch with Merv, the waiter comes over and says, 'May I take your order?' and Merv says, 'Ooo! "May I take your order?" What a great puzzle.' And he writes it down."

—Pat Sajak, host of WHEEL OF FORTUNE

"When this game is being played and a celebrity sits down for $10,000 and says things that are hot, what we really want to happen is for some woman at home in Peoria to say, 'the sun, Florida, Africa, a match.' If we can get her to talk to the TV screen, we've succeeded."

—Producer Bob Stewart of THE $10,000 PYRAMID

"We've tried to pick girls who are not just stunning, but who might look like the girl next door—or at least the way you'd like the girl next door to look."

—Jay Wolpert, host of THE PRICE IS RIGHT

"Add the Bible as a category and I will show you how to win $64,000."

> —Mrs. Catherine Kreitzer, an excerpt from the letter
> she submitted to get on THE $64,000 QUESTION

"I know I wasn't stupid, but when I finished the show I wasn't sure."

> —George Fenneman, announcer on YOU BET YOUR LIFE

"If a newlywed couple loved and respected each other, they probably would never have thought about doing the show in the first place. And even if they had, we would most likely not have selected them for the program. They would have made lousy contestants."

> —Chuck Barris on THE NEWLYWED GAME

"What a terrible thing to do to the American public."

> —President Eisenhower on the Quiz Show Scandals

"That show came back to haunt me many times. It was not my favorite."

—Mark Goodson, producer of BEAT THE CLOCK

"There's something about the guy that worries me."

—Bob Edwards, contestant coordinator for PRESS YOUR LUCK,
to producer Bill Carruthers on bringing
contestant Paul Larson on the show

"I discovered there were only six patterns on the board. It wasn't random and so it was just a process of memorizing the patterns."

—Paul Larson, winner of $110,237 on PRESS YOUR LUCK
(Single appearance all-time winner)

"I should have listened to Bob."

—Bill Carruthers, producer of PRESS YOUR LUCK

"Sure, *Queen* was vulgar and sleazy and filled with bathos and bad taste. That was why it was so successful." —Howard Blake, producer of QUEEN FOR A DAY

"My absolutely firm feelings about reality on TV is that there's too little of it. The greatest things are the real things you see—baseball, football, conventions— where the unexpected is ahead of you and you're interested. I wanted to set up an event where people would be tremendously interested, would care what happened, and not know until it happened what was going to happen."

—Louis G. Cowan, producer of THE $64,000 QUESTION and President of CBS Television

"The rigging took place not so much to feed them the questions and answers but to introduce some drama into the shows." —Dan Enright, creator of TWENTY ONE

"How well can I communicate with just one word?"

—Bob Stewart, creator of PASSWORD

"Chuck (Barris) told me early on that the reason why there are three guys and one gal was because for years, women stayed home and waited for guys to call. Wouldn't that be neat, women could sit home and say 'I'll take him...'"

—Jim Lange, emcee of THE DATING GAME

"We refuse to accept the sorry excuse that the actions of the quiz show producers are merely symbolic of our nation's preoccupation with material wealth. Honesty and truth still are respected above easy money in America. And the proof is in the fact that viewers *are* angry because of the dishonesty now revealed."

—From a *TV Guide* editorial, January 1960

"People haven't changed one bit. They're all exactly the same. Human nature doesn't change, the desire to win doesn't change. Everybody loves to get loot."

—Dennis James, emcee EMERITUS

"Creating a game isn't like conceiving a drama... In games you begin with a blank page. It's almost like trying to create a new sport. Think of a new sport. Think of how few new sports really come along."

—Mark Goodson, producer

"In my day the emcee . . . had to carry the show. There were very few electronic devices, no flashing lights, everything was interviews and excitement building up. Today everything is electronic. They don't need an emcee anymore. If they blow a fuse, they have no show."

—Bert Parks, emcee

"I apologize for insulting your intelligence. From now on, I promise to stick to comedy"

—Jackie Gleason to the CBS TV audience as he canceled his own show, YOU'RE IN THE PICTURE on the air, February 3, 1961

"It was developed prior to the days of talk shows. So LINE was more than a game. It was an elegant talk show plus a game."

—Mark Goodson on WHAT'S MY LINE

"It's an easy game that everyone of all ages can play and enjoy at the same time. A two-year-old can sit and enjoy watching the wheel spin. I get all kinds of letters from people saying their child learned the alphabet from watching the show."

—Vanna White, hostess on WHEEL OF FORTUNE

"I'm producing RICH for the benefit of Mr. America, the poor guy who works all day, comes home, eats his dinner, goes into the living room and puts on his slippers. This guy doesn't want a *Studio One* or some arty show. He's looking for LUCY or RICH. He has simple elemental tastes. If I don't put on a real needy case, I get a dirty, nasty letter from Mr. America."

—Walt Farmer, producer of STRIKE IT RICH

"But $64,000 gets into the realm of the possible."

—Louis G. Cowan, producer of THE $64,000 QUESTION
on how much money was enough to attract an audience

"What we did was wrong, we misled the people, we misled the viewers, we betrayed their trust. We did it because we thought it was a form of entertainment. In an effort to provide better entertainment we lost sight of what we were doing. I will never lie again. It's not worth it. I'll simply tell the truth and bear the consequences."   —Dan Enright, creator of TWENTY-ONE
commenting on the rigging scandals of the 50's

"Why don't you do a show where you give the contestants the answer?"   —Julann Griffin
to then-husband Merv Griffin on the idea for JEOPARDY!

"Sure, and I'll end up in the slammer."
—Merv to Julann

Quiz 5: The Great Game Show Oddities Quiz

With The Answers Included

1. What southwestern town actually changed its name in order to get one of the greatest game shows of all time to broadcast there?
Hot Springs, New Mexico changed its name to TRUTH OR CONSEQUENCES. Smart move.

2. A former Tarzan hosted a musical game show. Who was he?
Ron Ely swung in from the jungle to host FACE THE MUSIC.

3. A short-lived quiz show premiered on CBS in the summer of 1953. Another quiz show which became one of the most successful in the history of television premiered on NBC in 1975. They had nothing in common except their name. What was it?
WHEEL OF FORTUNE. The 1953 version was a sobber that rewarded good Samaritans for their good deeds by allowing them to tell their tale and then spin a wheel and collect a reward. The 1975 version continues to make television history; the 1953 version was history in less than six months. Good just doesn't have the staying power of greed.

4. **Two game shows have the distinction of airing on the four networks in existence during their time on the air. What are their names?**
PANTOMIME QUIZ. *Between 1950 and 1963 it was broadcast by ABC, NBC, CBS, and DUMONT.*
DOWN YOU GO *hit all four between 1951 and 1956.*

5. **What are $712.05 for prime-time and $516.32 for daytime?**
With the addition of a Golden Gong , the figures are the prizes for GONG SHOW *winners.*

6. **What President and First Lady may win the prize for all-time game show fans? Hint: They were nuts for** WHAT'S MY LINE?.
Dwight and Mamie Eisenhower were such fans during their White House days that, at their request, tapes of the show were flown down to Augusta, Georgia, several times when they missed the show on the air.

7. **A famous comedy team of the 50s and 60s was the only standup duo to host a game show. Who were they?**
Bob and Ray. The team was extremely popular as writers and humorists and appeared regularly on television as well as gracing the pages of Mad *magazine.*

8. **Another duo, even more famous, however, did a parody of the $64,000** QUESTION **during the rigging scandals on the** *Colgate Comedy Hour* **that really hit the mark. Who were they?**
Dean Martin and Jerry Lewis.

9. **What 1986 game show hosted by Jim Lange offered the richest prize in game show history as well as perhaps the longest title?**
THE ONE MILLION DOLLAR CHANCE OF A LIFETIME.

10. What 1975 show allowed three teams to compete for a full week before deciding the winner?
THREE FOR THE MONEY with Dick Enberg.

11. The original name of TO TELL THE TRUTH lasted only through the first week. What was it?
NOTHING BUT THE TRUTH.

12. What was the only game show to be shot entirely on film and edited into 30 minute segments to air both on radio and television? Also, why?
YOU BET YOUR LIFE was filmed in one-hour segments and edited to capture the best of Groucho and also to have a little control over the more risqué side of the master's humor.

13. Four successful game shows spent their final years broadcasting from the gaming capitol of the world—Lost Wages, Nevada. OK, Las Vegas. What were they?
LET'S MAKE A DEAL. HOLLYWOOD SQUARES. DEALER'S CHOICE. LAS VEGAS GAMBIT.

14. Come up with the number of years on radio, network television, and syndication that made TRUTH OR CONSEQUENCES the longest running game show in history. (Not consecutive)
37 years. 1940–1987. So it's a tough one. So what?

15. Sure Robert Strom won a lot of money, so did Dr. Brothers, but it took them many appearances to do it. The all-time, single appearance, money winner was an unemployed Ice Cream Truck driver from Lebanon, Ohio. Who was he, how much did he win, and what was the show?
On May 19, 1984, Paul Larson won $110,237 on a show called PRESS YOUR LUCK. He had a streak of 45 consecutive hits on the big board without a "Whammie." And he did it legally.

To Tell The Truth...or else

In the category of "some people will do anything to be on television" falls HOT SEAT, a 1976 ABC event in which a husband took a lie detector test at the end of the game to determine whether or not he had been telling the truth.

16. AMERICA'S MOST WANTED has nothing on WHAT'S MY LINE?. John Daly and the panel were responsible for catching a crook long before it was popular. What happened?
An elephant trainer appearing on the show was recognized by a Michigan viewer as a wanted car thief; he walked off the show into the arms of the law.

17. Who is the only game show host to have a city park named after him?
Ralph Edwards Park is in Truth or Consequences, New Mexico.

18. Bill Cullen is the "host with the most" in terms of the number of different game shows he's emceed. How many?
Twenty-four.

19. Tom Kennedy has an equally famous brother and a different real name. Who is his brother and what is his real name?
His brother is Jack Narz and, of course, that's his real last name. He changed on his brother's suggestion when he left his job as a radio announcer in Kentucky and came north to seek his fortune.

20. **Capt. Thom McKee holds the record for most money ever won on a game show and the record for the number of return appearances. How much, how long and what show?** *Over $300,000 in 47 straight returns on TIC-TAC-DOUGH.*

21. **Groucho always did his best to see that his contestants won something. What was his favorite question to the losers?** *Who was buried in Grant's Tomb?*

22. **The theme music for JEOPARDY! has a name and a composer. What is the name and who is the composer?** *The name of the tune is* **A Tune For Tony.** *The composer is JEOPARDY! creator Merv Griffin.*

Norman 'Concentration' Blumenthal's recipe for a game show:

4 contestants (vary with type of show)
165 pounds of ham (emcee brand)
150 pounds of announcer (deep-voice type)
250 good-natured people in audience (all shapes)
1 ton of prizes (best available)
Some cheesecake (2 gorgeous female models)
1 cup of humor (very dry)
1 cup of pathos (very wet)
Dash of greed
Dash of laughter (canned or live)
1/2 teaspoon game

THE GERITOL REPORT
—1994

17

Alex Trebek—
We Think We'll Keep Him

Geritol, the vitamin supplement that sponsored the scandal-ridden TWENTY-ONE in the 1950s, isn't afraid to look at its past. In fact, to mark the 1994 opening of Robert Redford's movie *Quiz Show,* which recounted the story of the scandals, the tonic makers decided to have a look at game shows past and present. Their conclusion? Viewers and critics may long for television's "good old days," but not, by and large, when it comes to game shows.

In a specially commissioned survey, the company found viewers believe today's shows are more credible, more challenging, more entertaining—and have better prizes. Among the findings:

Hosts' Honesty (scale of 10)

◆ **Alex Trebek**	JEOPARDY	8.6
◆ **Bob Barker**	THE PRICE IS RIGHT	7.1
◆ **Pat Sajak**	WHEEL OF FORTUNE	7.1

Host most likely to take Geritol

◆ **Bob Barker**

Hosts' Overall Geritol Rating (50 possible points)

- ◆ **Alex Trebek**   41
- ◆ **Bob Barker**   38
- ◆ **Pat Sajak**   36

Favorite Show

- ◆ **Jeopardy!**   38 PERCENT
- ◆ **Wheel of Fortune**   29 PERCENT
- ◆ **The Price is Right**   18 PERCENT

The hosts' overall Geritol rating combines scores for honesty, personality, intelligence, wardrobe and sex appeal. Alex Trebek received top scores in all categories.

Winning The Biggest Game Of All

Jay Wolpert of Glen Cove, N.Y., was a world champion on JEOPARDY!... and went on to become a producer of THE NEW PRICE IS RIGHT and a developer of other game shows.

Host Peter Tomarken of PRESS YOUR LUCK in 1983. Pete is one of the movers and shakers behind the Game Show Channel which is now broadcasting on Direct Television and will hopefully soon find a place on regular cable.

A TRUE STORY!

18

Paul Larson's Amazing Experience or, Why it Pays to Pay Attention

This is a story of the American Dream fulfilled, of how a quiet and unassuming man from the great hinterlands stunned the network Goliaths and walked away with a fortune.

Usually, Paul Larson drove an ice cream truck in Lebanon, Ohio but in November of 1983, he was out of work. For the majority of Americans in Lebanon, a container of *Mister Softee* doesn't constitute a cold weather treat. It followed that Paul had a lot of time on his hands during the winter months. So it was that he found himself watching a lot of daytime television, particularly game shows, which he loved.

Like millions of Americans in 1983, a new entry from CBS caught his eye. It was called PRESS YOUR LUCK. LUCK was truly a game show of the 80s, the action was fast and frantic and the stakes were high. The lights flashed, the buzzers buzzed, the audience screamed, the contestants screamed louder than the audience, the host, Peter Tomarken, had to scream to be heard. Everybody was having a great time.

The concept was simple, basic game show. The first part involved three contestants answering questions to win spins on the big board. In part two, contestants used their spins to win cash and prizes. But, potential disaster loomed in the form of dreaded *whammies*. *Whammies* were nasty little creatures that lived hidden on certain squares and if you landed on one of them you lost everything. The lights revealed them as they moved around the board, but so quickly that they were hard to see. The contestants pressed a plunger hoping to stop the lights on squares that contained big bucks, not the gruesome little nebbishes that would rob them of their hard-earned cash. At anytime, they could pass spins to an opponent (who had to take them) or they could *Press* their luck.

So Paul watched. As winter dragged on, he realized something. The whammies moved in patterns. He began to videotape the show and freeze the frame to study the board. He was right, there were only six patterns in which whammie's appeared. It wasn't random; all he had to do was memorize six sets and he would be the perfect Presser. He tried it out. It worked. He was winning thousands sitting on his couch. Paul became obsessed with getting on the show. There was, however, a slight problem. The pot of gold was in Los Angeles and Paul was broke in Lebanon, Ohio.

He had no choice. Paul scrounged the money to get a ticket to LA. He auditioned and the producer, Bill Carruthers, loved him. Paul was the ultimate contestant. He was charming, eager, played the game extremely well and he was out of work. It didn't get any better than that. The audience would love him. The contestant coordinator, Bob Edwards, was wary, but the producer wanted him. Paul was booked for a taping.

At the end of the first round, Paul was in third place. He was doing OK, not great. But he knew something no one else did. He knew the patterns. All he wanted was a chance to spin. For Paul, it wasn't a question of pressing his luck, it was opportunity knocking. And when he got his chance, Paul answered the door.

Early in the second round, a correct answer earned Paul a spin. He went on a wild ride that opened Pandora's Box, sent waves of panic through the control room and started executive phones ringing all over LA. The guy couldn't miss and nobody could figure out why. The odds were 1 in 6 that he had to blow it. There was no way he should have been able to keep going, but if he was cheating no one could figure out how. The show was into its second half hour and still he hadn't hit a whammie. The execs made their decision. They would keep the tape rolling and investigate for potential fraud later. No one could afford to have PRESS YOUR LUCK become the TWENTY-ONE of the 90s.

Paul Larson hit the plunger 45 straight times and 45 straight times he won money. On the 45th he was out of spins, but a disgruntled opponent with no chance to win passed her spins to him. The tension in the studio was unbelievable. Paul was drained but he had no choice, the rules said he had to take the spin. Spin number 46 was a winner and Paul stopped. He had won $110,237 in cash and prizes and set a record for the most money ever won in a single appearance on a game show.

The lawyers looked into the situation and decided that Paul hadn't cheated, he had just paid attention. Paul got his money, went back to Ohio and took his place in game show history. The computer programmers went immediately to work to make sure nothing like that could happen again.

A footnote: Paul's amazing experience aired on May 19, 1984 as a full hour. It's still around and showing occasionally on the USA Network as a rerun.

You Tell 'em "Chuckie Baby"

Chuck Barris says, and we quote:

"The DATING and NEWLYWED games are stupid, mawkish, but never harmful. Daytime TV does not make meaningful statements. You begin and end with the banal. I know what the elements are. Emotions and tensions. You must bring out those hidden hostilities in your contestants. You can actually watch them temporarily lose their sanity on the air. Thus audiences are being entertained either in awe or shock or horror or joy over someone going bananas in public."

A Game Show Who's Who

The Producers

Chuck Barris

While most game show producers usually remain behind the scenes, 'Chuckie Baby' Barris became a household name as the obnoxious host of NBC's THE GONG SHOW in 1976. Barris launched his television career with Dick Clark's AMERICAN BANDSTAND, and briefly served as vice-president of daytime programming for ABC. In 1965, he sealed the future of Chuck Barris Productions by updating the 1949 version of BLIND DATE with a new game show, THE DATING GAME, an instant daytime hit that was soon added to prime-time scheduling. Barris followed immediately with THE NEWLYWED GAME, an incredible success that pushed the beloved PASSWORD off the air.

Shows:

THE DATING GAME
THE NEWLYWED GAME
DREAM GIRL OF 1967
THE FAMILY GAME
HOW'S YOUR MOTHER-IN-LAW
THE BABY GAME
THE PARENT GAME
TREASURE HUNT
THREE'S A CROWD
CAMOUFLAGE

Chuck Barris and the famous gong.

Jack Barry & Dan Enright

From reigning as kings of the quiz shows when they launched TWENTY-ONE in 1956, Jack Barry and Dan Enright fell from grace during the game show scam after Charles Van Doren admitted being coached for their show. Barry, a former handkerchief salesman, hooked up with Enright at WOR in New York. They introduced WINKY DINK AND YOU, an interactive kid's show that encouraged young viewers to draw pictures on their TV screens. The dynamic duo hit the top of quiz show ratings in 1957 with TWENTY-ONE. Following the scandals, no networks would touch them and Enright moved to Canada. Barry sold THE JOKER'S WILD to CBS in 1972, and then reunited with his former partner to revamp the old TIC TAC DOUGH.

Shows:

JUVENILE JURY
LIFE BEGINS AT EIGHTY
TIC TAC DOUGH
TWENTY-ONE
YOU'RE ON YOUR OWN
HIGH-LOW
CONCENTRATION
DOUGH RE MI
THE REEL GAME
JOKER'S WILD

HOLLYWOOD'S TALKING
BLANK CHECK
BREAK THE BANK
HOLLYWOOD CONNECTION
NEW TIC TAC DOUGH
BULLSEYE
PLAY THE PERCENTAGES
JOKER JOKER JOKER
HOT POTATO

A Producing Fool

With the debut of THE REEL GAME in 1971, Jack Barry gained the distinction of having been involved in the creation of over 30 shows.

Louis G. Cowan

One morning in 1955, Louis G. Cowan, a quiz show packager and originator of the radio hits QUIZ KIDS and STOP THE MUSIC, came up with the idea for a new show. Six months later, he premiered THE $64,000 QUESTION, an instant hit. Everything that the father of the big money quiz touched seemingly turned to gold. Cowan left THE $64,000 QUESTION only a few months after it aired and went to work at CBS, where he served as president when the game show scandal broke in 1958. Cowan steadfastly denied knowledge of game rigging, but CBS forced him to resign. He never produced another quiz show. Instead, Cowan ran the journalism department at Columbia University and started the *Columbia Journalism Review*.

Shows:

QUIZ KIDS
KAY KYSER'S KOLLEGE OF MUSICAL KNOWLEDGE
STOP THE MUSIC
REMEMBER THE DATE
WHAT'S MY NAME?
DOWN YOU GO
ASK ME ANOTHER
BALANCE YOUR BUDGET
THE $64,000 QUESTION

NBC's in-house producer Noah, and independent producer Enright's TIC-TAC-DOUGH, the show that Charles Van Doren first wanted to be on.

Ralph Edwards

Ralph Edwards is synonymous with two of the most popular television shows of all times, *This Is Your Life* and TRUTH OR CONSEQUENCES. He simultaneously hosted both shows. *This Is Your Life* won back-to-back Emmys for BEST AUDIENCE PARTICIPATION SHOW in 1953 and '54. TRUTH OR CONSEQUENCES, created by Edwards, aired on the radio in 1950 and became the longest running show in broadcast history. He emceed the early shows but captured a loyal television audience when he hired an unknown disk jockey named Bob Barker. As a publicity stunt, the town of Hot Springs, New Mexico changed its name to Truth or Consequences in 1950. A street, park and wing of the local museum in the town are named for Ralph Edwards.

Shows:

TRUTH OR CONSEQUENCES
PLACE THE FACE
IT COULD BE YOU
END OF THE RAINBOW
ABOUT FACES
CROSS WITS
THE NEW NAME THAT TUNE
KNOCKOUT
SO YOU THINK YOU'VE GOT TROUBLES

I Just Like To Help...

HAVE A HEART which premiered on the Dumont network in 1954 may be the most giving game show in TV history. The winners actually turned the money over to charities of their choice.

Ralph Edwards before the cameras on Truth or Consequences.

Mark Goodson & Bill Todman

Anyone who has ever watched television game shows can certainly recite the line, *"This has been a Mark Goodson, Bill Todman production."* When the unlikely duo teamed up in 1946 to sell the radio quiz WINNER TAKES ALL, they were destined to become kings of the game shows. Goodson, an introverted kid from a poor family, headed to New York after finishing law school at San Francisco State University. He soon met Todman, an urbane young man from a wealthy New York family. They struck the jackpot with such hits as WHAT'S MY LINE?, THE PRICE IS RIGHT, PASSWORD, and FAMILY FEUD. Mark Goodson Productions continues to produce TV game shows, including several televised lottery games. The company earned a spot in the *Guinness Book of World Records* for the most television shows produced: more than 39,000 episodes.

Shows:

WINNER TAKES ALL	CALL MY BLUFF
BEAT THE CLOCK	IT'S YOUR MOVE
WHAT'S MY LINE?	SNAP JUDGMENT
IT'S NEWS TO ME	HE SAID, SHE SAID
THE NAME'S THE SAME	CONCENTRATION
I'VE GOT A SECRET	NOW YOU SEE IT
TWO FOR THE MONEY	FAMILY FEUD
JUDGE FOR YOURSELF	TATTLETALES
FEATHER YOUR NEST	SHOWOFFS
THE PRICE IS RIGHT	THE BETTER SEX
TO TELL THE TRUTH	CARD SHARKS
PLAY YOUR HUNCH	MINDREADERS
SPLIT PERSONALITY	BLOCKBUSTERS
NUMBER PLEASE	CHILD'S PLAY
PASSWORD	MATCH GAME/HOLLYWOOD
SAY WHEN	SQUARES HOUR
THE MATCH GAME	BODY LANGUAGE
MISSING LINKS	TRIVIA TRAP
GET THE MESSAGE	

Merv Griffin

The consummate entertainer and one of the richest men in the business, Merv Griffin has done it all. Starting out as a singer, he became familiar to television game show audiences in the 1950s as a recurring guest, host, and panelist. In 1959, Goodson-Todman hired Griffin to host PLAY YOUR HUNCH. His success led to an afternoon talk show, and in 1963 NBC allowed him to produce and host WORD FOR WORD. That marked the start of Merv Griffin Enterprises, which Coca-Cola bought for a reported $250 million in 1986. Griffin's biggest successes came in 1964 when he premiered JEOPARDY!, and again in 1974 when WHEEL OF FORTUNE hit the airwaves and became the highest-rated syndicated show of all time.

Shows:

WORD FOR WORD
JEOPARDY!
LET'S PLAY POST OFFICE
ONE IN A MILLION
REACH FOR THE STARS
THE MEMORY GAME
WHEEL OF FORTUNE
HEADLINE CHASERS

My Mind Is Always Working, Even When I'm Out Of The Office

Merv Griffin, with the help of his wife, dreamed up JEOPARDY! on a red-eye flight from Los Angeles to New York.

Merrill Heatter & Bob Quigley

In the 1950s, daytime television ushered in a new crop of game show packagers. Merrill Heatter, a former writer for YOU ARE THERE, and Bob Quigley, a comedy writer for Victor Borge, joined forces to produce the first show after the Fifties scandal. Billed as rig-proof, VIDEO VILLAGE debuted as an oversized, trendy video board game and introduced Monty Hall to America. Heatter's and Quigley's novelty environments became their hallmark. They produced a pinball show, MAGNIFICENT MARBLE MACHINE, and made a game of the lie detector test, HOT SEAT. Then they updated tic-tac-toe with celebrities and called it THE HOLLYWOOD SQUARES. They sold the entire company to Filmways (later Orion Pictures) for $10 million.

Shows:

VIDEO VILLAGE	GAMBIT
DOUBLE EXPOSURE	AMATEUR'S GUIDE TO LOVE
PEOPLE WILL TALK	BAFFLE
THE CELEBRITY GAME	HIGH ROLLERS
SHENANIGANS	THE MAGNIFICENT MARBLE
SHOWDOWN	MACHINE
P.D.Q.	HOT SEAT
THE HOLLYWOOD SQUARES	TO SAY THE LEAST
EVERYBODY'S TALKING	BEDTIME STORIES
TEMPTATION	BATTLESTARS
FUNNY YOU SHOULD ASK	FANTASY
NAME DROPPERS	THE ALL-STAR BLITZ
RUNAROUND	BARGAIN HUNTER

Bob Stewart

Stewart built a career out of word games and created two of the most popular game shows on television, PASSWORD and THE $10,000 PYRAMID. A former comedy sketch writer for WNBC radio, Stewart moved over to WNBC-TV in 1954 where he produced an early stunt game show. Stewart then invented two shows, THE PRICE IS RIGHT and NOTHING BUT THE TRUTH (later renamed TO TELL THE TRUTH), but couldn't sell them to a sponsor. Goodson-Todman, however, picked them up and hired Stewart as the producer. In 1964, after PASSWORD, the first show to pair celebrities and civilians, became the highest rated daytime game show ever Stewart struck out on his own. He produced a number of other shows but not another hit until 1973 with PYRAMID.

Shows:

EYE GUESS
THE FACE IS FAMILIAR
PERSONALITY
YOU'RE PUTTING ME ON
THREE ON A MATCH
THE $10,000 ($20,000 $25,000 $50,000 $100,000)PYRAMID
JACKPOT!
WINNING STREAK
BLANKETY BLANKS
SHOOT FOR THE STARS
LOVE EXPERTS
PASS THE BUCK
CHAIN REACTION
GO!
DOUBLE TALK

WHERE IN THE WORLD...?

This One's a Runaway Hit

Where will game shows turn up next? Would you believe . . . The Public Broadcasting System?

That's right. WHERE IN THE WORLD IS CARMEN SANDIEGO? a hit children's television game show inspired by the fabulously popular series of children's educational software programs, began on PBS in 1990.

The television show's premise is the same as that of the software: to teach geography to children aged 6 to 13 by giving them clues that identify places around the world as they chase the sneaky criminal Carmen. Winner of both Emmy and Peabody awards, (CARMEN was nominated for seven daytime Emmys in 1993 alone) the show is a co-production of WQED in Pittsburgh and WGBH in Boston.

A few facts for Carmen chasers:

Contestants are aided by a cadre of celebrity clue-givers including:

◆ Olympic figure skaters Scott Hamilton, Kristi Yamaguchi, and Kitty and Peter Carruthers

◆ Senator Ted Kennedy

◆ Singer/actor David Cassidy

◆ *Today* show host Katie Couric

◆ Ahmad Rashad and Willow Bay of NBA's *Inside Stuff*

- Shari Lewis and Lambchop
- Talk show hosts including Sally Jesse Raphael, Geraldo Rivera and Maury Povich

Teachers like Carmen, too:

- 98 percent of respondents to an independent survey said CARMEN is as good or better than other children's programs.
- Over 40 percent use broadcasts or videotapes in class.
- 81 percent said the show is very or extremely useful in teaching geography.

Host Greg Lee and contestants on PBS's WHERE IN THE WORLD IS CARMEN SANDIEGO?

Quiz 6: The More the Merrier

The Spin-Off Quiz

1. Can you name three shows starting with the letter "D" that required contestants to recognize a person, place or thing from a drawing?

2. There haven't been many women hosting game shows. Name the show and its hostess that spawned THE NEWLYWED GAME. Hint: It was on the Dumont Network back in 1954.

3. First there was PASSWORD then there were three other versions. Name them.

4. OK. Do the same for THE $10,000 PYRAMID but you have to name four.

5. PEOPLE ARE FUNNY with lovable Art Linkletter was so hot that four of its segments were the genesis of hit game shows of their own. Name them.

6. Harry Salter, a big band leader, conceived and produced the first musical quiz show and one of its successful spin-offs. Name the two shows.

7. What is the name of the saturday morning children's television game show that was spun off from a regular game show? What is the name of the original? The kiddy concept had a short run on NBC in 1968. Hint: The nine celebrities were costumed as storybook characters. Go ahead and name the host as well.

8. THE DATING GAME was based on a show that shared a four year run on ABC and Dumont from 1949 to 1953. The first female host emceed the show which featured six men competing for a date with a gorgeous model. What was the show and who was the host?

(Answers on page 280)

For the Big Bucks ($32,000)

Date: August 2, 1955
Show: THE $64,000 QUESTION
Host: Hal March
Contestant: Gino Prato, a shoemaker from Brooklyn, N.Y.
Category: Grand Opera

Questions:

A. Name the Giuseppe Verdi opera which started Arturo Toscanini on his career as a conductor.
B. Name the country where Toscanini conducted this opera.
C. Name the city where the original opera premiered.
D. On the eve of what holiday was the premiere?

Answers:

A. *Aida*
B. Brazil
C. Cairo
D. Christmas

22

What It Takes To Be a "Stud"

We came across a contract and release from the producers of Fox's
STUDS , circa 1992. It had to be signed by all potential contestants. You
think the IRS is tough? Take a look at this:

I acknowledge that I have been advised and
informed that STUDS is a talk show about relationships, and
that the program will be structured as follows: Two men will
go out on dates with the same three women, following
which, the women will compare notes on the two men and
select the "bigger stud."

I acknowledge that I have been advised and
informed that you have not screened the background of
any of the individuals selected to be my dates so as to
determine whether such individuals have any medical or
health problems, a criminal record, or a propensity for
criminal or antisocial behavior. In this regard, I understand
that it is my responsibility to arrange a meeting place and
activity on each of my dates that will minimize the risk of
the types of harm that may occur in the course of social
encounters of this nature. These risks include, but are in no
way limited to: non-consensual physical contact; commu-
nicable sexual diseases; personal injury or property dam-

age; permanent disability or death; emotional distress; invasion of privacy; slander; and libel.

I have been informed and I fully understand that the advice given to me by the host of the program is intended to be for entertainment only. Should I decide to follow all or any part of such advice, this decision shall be entirely at my own risk.

STUDS host Mark De Carlo enjoys a little double-entendre between the Studs and Studettes.

Serious Stats

In the 14 1/2 years Norman Blumenthal produced CONCENTRATION...
- there were 3,796 half-hour broadcasts or
- 79 straight days, if aired non-stop
- if aired 1/2 hour per week as nighttime shows, that's 73 years; starting with the 1958 premiere, the show would run through August 2031
- 22,031 commercials
- 9 million feet of videotape
- The show had 7,592 winners, who received:
- 512 cars
- 268 travel and camp trailers
- 397 boats
- 1,287 trips (domestic and overseas)
- 12 trips around the world
- 857 furs
- other merchandise and cash worth over $10 million

JUST THE FACTS, MA'AM...

1975—A Banner Year For the Correct Answer

The record for the most game shows on the air in a single season was achieved in 1975. Some were hits, some were misses; but either way, it's clear that America was obsessed with the right answer in the mid-70s. Maybe Watergate had something to do with it.

At any rate, here are the 26 shows that crammed the pages of *TV Guide* the year the Miami Dolphins won Super Bowl VIII.

THE BIG SHOWDOWN
CELEBRITY SWEEPSTAKES
CONCENTRATION
CROSS-WITS
DIAMOND HEAD GAME
GAMBIT
HIGH ROLLERS
THE HOLLYWOOD SQUARES
JACKPOT
JEOPARDY!
THE JOKER'S WILD
LET'S MAKE A DEAL
LIAR'S CLUB

MATCH GAME '75
MONEY MAZE
NAME THAT TUNE
NOW YOU SEE IT
PASSWORD'S ALL-STARS
THE PRICE IS RIGHT
SPLIT SECOND
TATTLETALES
THE $10,000 PYRAMID
TO TELL THE TRUTH
TREASURE HUNT
WHAT'S MY LINE?
WINNING STREAK

QUIZ 7: WHERE HAVE I HEARD THAT?...

24

Match The Famous Tag Lines With The Shows

See Page 280 for the answers

Tag Lines

A. _____   "Numbers 5 and 2."

B. _____   "50, 50, joker."

C. _____   "Hello, stars."

D. _____   "Sign in, please."

E. _____   "Number one, what is your name, please?"

F. _____   "Watch out for the bankrupt."

G. _____   "Any 21 wins our jackpot."

H. _____   "And the secret word is..."

I. _____   "Come on down!"

J. _____   "Is it bigger than a breadbox?"

188

Shows

1. WHAT'S MY LINE?

2. YOU BET YOUR LIFE

3. I'VE GOT A SECRET

4. TO TELL THE TRUTH

5. THE PRICE IS RIGHT

6. CONCENTRATION

7. HOLLYWOOD SQUARES

8. WHEEL OF FORTUNE

9. JOKER'S WILD

10. GAMBIT

THE BEST AND
THE BRIGHTEST...

25

All The Emmys
Ever Awarded Game Shows
Through 1994

The annual Emmy Awards, presented by the National Academy of Television Arts and Sciences, were designed to honor excellence in television broadcasting. But they also reflect American viewers' changing tastes. In early years, categories changed almost yearly, as television experimented with different types of programming.

Beginning with the award for Most Popular Program in the first year the Emmys were given, the wildly popular game and quiz shows of the 1950s captured frequent awards—until scandals pushed them off the air late in the decade. Struggling to make a comeback and still competing with prime-time programming, game shows captured only one award in the 1960s. Until the Daytime Emmy Awards were begun in 1974, the gamers were profitable but forgotten when it came to sharing praise.

Emmy Awards

Most Popular Television Program

1948   PANTOMIME QUIZ (KTLA)

Best Game and Audience Participation Show

1950   TRUTH OR CONSEQUENCES   (KTTV, CBS)

Most Outstanding Personality

1950   Groucho Marx   (KNBH, NBC)

Best Audience Participation, Quiz, or Panel Program

1952	WHAT'S MY LINE?	(CBS)
1953	WHAT'S MY LINE?	(CBS)
1954	WHAT'S MY LINE?	(CBS)
1955	THE $64,000 QUESTION	(CBS)
1958–59	WHAT'S MY LINE?	(CBS)

Outstanding Program Achievement in the Field of Panel, Quiz, or Audience Participation

1962–63   THE G.E. COLLEGE BOWL   (CBS)

Daytime Emmy Awards

First presented in May 1974, this category of awards was created, according to NBC Vice President Lin Bolen, so that daytime viewers and performers would "finally get their proper reward."

Outstanding Game or Audience Participation Show

1973–74   PASSWORD, FRANK WAYNE, EXECUTIVE PRODUCER; HOWARD FELSER, PRODUCER   (ABC)

1974–75   THE HOLLYWOOD SQUARES, Merrill Heatter, Bob Quigley, executive producers; Jay Redack, producer   (NBC)

1975–76   THE $20,000 PYRAMID, Bob Stewart, executive producer; Anne Marie Schmitt, producer   (ABC)

1976–77   FAMILY FEUD, Howard Felser, producer   (ABC)

1977–78   THE HOLLYWOOD SQUARES, Merrill Heatter, Bob Quigley, executive producers; Jay Redack, producer   (NBC)

1978–79   THE HOLLYWOOD SQUARES, Merrill Heatter, Bob Quigley, executive producers; Jay Redack, producer   (NBC)

1979–80   THE HOLLYWOOD SQUARES, Merrill Heatter, Bob Quigley, executive producers; Jay Redack, producer   (NBC)

THE $20,000 PYRAMID, Bob Stewart, executive producer; Anne Marie Schmitt, Jane Rothchild, producers   (ABC)

1980–81   THE $20,000 PYRAMID, Bob Stewart, executive producer; Anne Marie Schmitt, Jane Rothchild, producers   (ABC)

1981–82   PASSWORD PLUS, Robert Sherman, producer   (NBC)

1982–83	THE NEW $25,000 PYRAMID, Bob Stewart, executive producer; Anne Marie Schmitt, Sande Stewart, producers (CBS)
1983–84	THE $25,000 PYRAMID, Bob Stewart, executive producer (CBS)
1984–85	THE $25,000 PYRAMID, Bob Stewart, executive producer; Anne Marie Schmitt, producer (CBS)
1985–86	THE $25,000 PYRAMID, Bob Stewart, executive producer; Anne Marie Schmitt, producer (CBS)
1986–87	THE $25,000 PYRAMID, Bob Stewart, executive producer; Anne Marie Schmitt, supervising producer; David Michaels, Francine Bergman, producers (CBS)
1987–88	THE PRICE IS RIGHT, Frank Wayne, executive producer; Phillip Wayne, Roger Dubkowitz, producers (CBS)
1988–89	THE $25,000 PYRAMID, Bob Stewart, executive producer; Anne Marie Schmitt, supervising producer; Francine Bergman, David Michaels, producers (CBS)
1989–90	JEOPARDY!, Merv Griffin, executive producer; George Vosburgh, producer (syndicated)
1990–91	JEOPARDY!, Merv Griffin, executive producer; George Vosburgh, producer (syndicated)
1991–92	JEOPARDY!, Merv Griffin, executive producer; George Vosburgh, producer (syndicated)
1992–93	JEOPARDY!, Merv Griffin, executive producer; George Vosburgh, producer (syndicated)
1993–94	JEOPARDY!, Merv Griffin, executive producer; George Vosburgh, producer (syndicated)

Outstanding Host or Hostess in a Game Show

1973–74	Peter Marshall, THE HOLLYWOOD SQUARES (NBC)
1974–75	Peter Marshall, THE HOLLYWOOD SQUARES (NBC)
1975–76	Allen Ludden, PASSWORD (ABC)

1976–77	Bert Convy, TATTLETALES (CBS)
1977–78	Richard Dawson, FAMILY FEUD (ABC)
1978–79	Dick Clark, THE $20,000 PYRAMID (ABC)
1979–80	Peter Marshall, THE HOLLYWOOD SQUARES (NBC)
1980–81	Peter Marshall, THE HOLLYWOOD SQUARES (NBC)
1981–82	Bob Barker, THE PRICE IS RIGHT (CBS)
1982–83	Betty White, JUST MEN (NBC)
1983–84	Bob Barker, THE PRICE IS RIGHT (CBS)
1984–85	Dick Clark, THE $25,000 PYRAMID (CBS)
1985–86	Dick Clark, THE $25,000 PYRAMID (CBS)
1986–87	Bob Barker, THE PRICE IS RIGHT (CBS)
1987–88	Bob Barker, THE PRICE IS RIGHT (CBS)
1988–89	Alex Trebek, JEOPARDY! (syndicated)
1989–90	Alex Trebek, JEOPARDY! (syndicated)
	Bob Barker, THE PRICE IS RIGHT (CBS)
1990–91	Bob Barker, THE PRICE IS RIGHT (CBS)
1991–92	Bob Barker, THE PRICE IS RIGHT (CBS)
1992–93	Pat Sajak, WHEEL OF FORTUNE (NBC)
1993–94	Bob Barker, THE PRICE IS RIGHT (CBS)

Outstanding Individual Direction for a Game Show

1973–74	Mike Gargiulo, JACKPOT (NBC)
1974–75	Jerome Shaw, THE HOLLYWOOD SQUARES (NBC)
1975–76	Mike Gargiulo, THE $20,000 PYRAMID (ABC)
1976–77	Mike Gargiulo, THE $20,000 PYRAMID (ABC)
1977–78	Mike Gargiulo, THE $20,000 PYRAMID (ABC)
1978–79	Jerome Shaw, THE HOLLYWOOD SQUARES (NBC)
1979–80	Jerome Shaw, THE HOLLYWOOD SQUARES (NBC)
1980–81	Mike Gargiulo, THE $20,000 PYRAMID (ABC)
1981–82	Paul Alter, FAMILY FEUD (ABC)
1982–83	Mark Breslow, THE PRICE IS RIGHT (CBS)
1983–84	Mark Breslow, THE PRICE IS RIGHT (CBS)
1984–85	Mark Breslow, THE PRICE IS RIGHT (CBS)

1985–86	Dick Carson, WHEEL OF FORTUNE (NBC)
1986–87	Mark Breslow, THE PRICE IS RIGHT (CBS)
1987–88	Bruce Burmester, THE $25,000 PYRAMID (CBS)
1988–89	Dick Schneider, JEOPARDY! (syndicated)
1989–90	Joseph Behar, FUN HOUSE (syndicated)
1990–91	Dick Schneider, JEOPARDY! (syndicated)
1991–92	Dick Schneider, JEOPARDY! (syndicated)
1992–93	Kevin McCarthy, Dick Schneider, JEOPARDY! (syndicated)
1993–94	Bob Levy, AMERICAN GLADIATORS

Best Writing for a Game Show

| 1973–74 | Jay Redack, Harry Friedman, Harold Schneider, Gary Johnson, Steve Levitch, Rich Kellard, Rowby Goren; THE HOLLYWOOD SQUARES (NBC) |

Outstanding Achievement in Writing —Special Class

| 1990–91 | Harry Eisenberg, Steven Dorfman, Kathy Easterling, Frederik Pohl IV, Steve D. Tamerius, Debbie Griffin, Michelle Johnson, Carol Campbell, JEOPARDY! (syndicated) |
| 1993–94 | Terrence McDonnell, Steven Dorfman, Kathy Easterling, Debbie Griffin, Frederick Pohl, IV, Steve D. Tamerius, JEOPARDY! (syndicated) |

Outstanding Technical Direction, Electronic Camera and Video Control

1984–85   Ray Angona, technical director; Ted Morales, Keeth Lawrence, Martin Wagner, Joseph Arviza, electronic cameras; Allen Latter, video control, THE PRICE IS RIGHT   (CBS)

1988–89   Ray Angona, technical director; Joseph Arvizu, Cesar Cabriera, Keeth Lawrence, Martin Wagner, electronic camera; Allen Latter, video control, THE PRICE IS RIGHT   (CBS)

1989–90   Ray Angona, technical director; Jose Arvizu, Cesar Cabriera, Keeth Lawrence, Martin Wagner, electronic camera; Allen Latter, senior video, THE PRICE IS RIGHT   (CBS)

1990–91   Ray Angona, technical director; Jose Arvizu, Cesar Cabriera, Wayne Getchell, Keeth Lawrence, Martin Wagner, electronic camera; Allen Latter, video control, THE PRICE IS RIGHT   (CBS)

1992–93   Ray Angona, technical director; Jose Arvizu, Cesar Cabriera, Wayne Getchell, Martin Wagner, electronic camera; Allen Latter, senior video, THE PRICE IS RIGHT   (CBS)

Paging Mr. Rayburn

Gene Rayburn started his career in television as a lowly page at NBC's Rockefeller Studios in New York City. He went on to other things, as pages do. When he returned to NBC, it was as host of CHOOSE UP SIDES, which led to the phenomenal success of MATCH GAME and a great career.

Wink Was There

Wink Martindale knew Elvis Presley while they were both teenagers growing up in Memphis. Wink worked at the recording studio where Elvis cut his very first single, *That's All Right Mama*. The young men remained close personal friends throughout their careers.

WILL YOU LOOK AT THIS...

26

Celebrities You Never Thought You'd See Hosting a Game Show

AL CAPP

"Li'l Abner" cartoonist on the celebrity quiz show ANYONE CAN WIN, CBS, 1953.

JOHNNY CARSON

WHO DO YOU TRUST?, CBS 1956–57 and ABC 1957–63 with sidekick Ed McMahon;
EARN YOUR VACATION, CBS 1954.

HANS CONRIED

MADE IN AMERICA, CBS, 1964.

WALTER CRONKITE

IT'S NEWS TO ME, CBS, 1951–54. (John Daly was also a host.)

JACKIE GLEASON

YOU'RE IN THE PICTURE, CBS, January 20, 1961.
Gleason canceled it after one broadcast.

MOSS HART (playwright)

ANSWER YES OR NO, NBC, 1950.

ERNIE KOVACS

Time Will Tell, DUMONT, 1954;
Take a Good Look, ABC 1959–61

OSCAR LEVANT

G.E. Guest House, CBS, 1951.

ED McMAHON

Missing Links, NBC, 1963–64, ABC, 1964
 (Dick Clark was also a host);
Concentration, NBC, 1958–73, syndication, 1973–79.
 (Other hosts Jack Barry, Hugh Downs, Bob Clayton,
 Art James, Bill Mazer, Jack Narz, Alex Trebek.)

JACK PAAR

Bank on the Stars, CBS, 1953, NBC, 1954.
 (Paar was followed by co-hosts Bill Cullen and Jimmy Nelson.)

TOM POSTON

Split Personality, CBS, 1959–60.

CARL REINER

The Celebrity Game, CBS, 1964–65, 1967–68.

ROD SERLING

Liar's Club, Syndication, 1969–70, 1974–80.

DICK VAN DYKE

Laugh Line and Mother's Day, NBC, 1959.

MIKE WALLACE

Guess Again, CBS, 1951;
The Big Surprise, NBC, 1955–57;
Who Pays?, NBC, 1959.

Not Just the Hits...

A Compendium of Game Shows from 1946 to 1995

Here are 50 years of quizzes, panels, stunts, sobs and everything else. We've complied an alphabetical listing of most of the game shows that have made it to the little screen, including the network they surfaced on, the year they premiered, a brief description, and the first host. Shows marked with an asterisk are described more fully in Chapter 5.

A

ABOUT FACES — ABC 1960

Contestants were given clues about each other's past. The winner was the first to match the clues with the correct opponent. Original host: Ben Alexander.

ACROSS THE BOARD — ABC 1959

Crossword game using pictures and words to complete a puzzle. Original host: Ted Brown.

ACT IT OUT— NBC 1949

Broadway actors competed in team charades. Original host: Bill Cullen.

THE AD-LIBBERS — ABC 1949

A team of actors (including a young Jack Lemmon) improvised stories based on viewer scenarios. Original host: John Dahl.

ALL ABOUT FACES — Syndication 1971

Celebrities teamed up to guess the outcome of a film clip. Original host: Richard Hayes.

THE ALL NEW DATING GAME— ABC 1986

See THE DATING GAME. Original host: Jeff MacGregor.

THE ALL NEW LET'S MAKE A DEAL — NBC 1990

See LET'S MAKE A DEAL. Original host: Monty Hall.

ALL STAR BLITZ — ABC 1985

THE HOLLYWOOD SQUARES with six instead of nine celebrities. Original host: Peter Marshall.

ALL-STAR SECRETS — ABC 1979

Current celebrity gossip. Original host: Bob Eubanks.

ALMOST ANYTHING GOES — ABC 1975

Three teams of contestants each representing their home towns competed in seven bizarre stunts for most total points. The show was run like a sporting event with on-field interviews by Dick Whittington and Regis Philbin. Based on BEAT THE CLOCK. Original host: Charlie Jones. Color commentator: Lynn Shakelford.

ALUMNI FUN — ABC 1963

Teams of college alumni answered lightweight questions for laughs. Original host: Peter Lind Hayes.

AMATEUR'S GUIDE TO LOVE — CBS 1972

A celebrity panel guessed the outcome of videos of contestants in suggestive or sexy situations. Original host: Gene Rayburn.

AMERICAN GLADIATORS* — Syndication 1989

The ultimate stunt/fantasy game. Contestants, two men and two women, who have to be in pretty good physical condition, go up against comic-book-style warriors, both male and female, in over-the-top battles on giant obstacle courses and suspended platforms. The warriors have names like: Nitro, Malibu, Blaze, and Lace, and their costumes fit their names. The Prize? $35,000 for making it through the entire season. Original host: Mike Adamle.

AMERICANA — NBC 1947

A studio quiz based on American history. Original host: Ben Grauer.

ANIMAL CRACK-UPS — ABC 1987

Kid-oriented, Saturday a.m. animal quiz. Original host: Alan Thicke.

THE ANNIVERSARY GAME — Syndication 1969

THE NEWLYWED GAME for couples with a few years of marriage behind them. Original host: Alan Hamel.

ANSWER YES OR NO — NBC 1950

Dilemmas, ethical or otherwise, were presented to contestants who had to decide how they would respond. A panel of celebs tried to guess how the contestants would answer. Original host: Moss Hart.

ANYBODY CAN PLAY — ABC 1958

George Fenneman got his chance to be Groucho in this spin-off of YOU BET YOUR LIFE. Original host: George Fenneman.

ANYONE CAN WIN — CBS 1953

Celebrity Q & A. Original host: Al Capp.

ANYTHING FOR MONEY — Syndication 1984

Using a *Candid Camera* format, this show captured on video the silly things people would do for money and exposed their follies to the viewing audience. Original host: Fred Travalena.

ANYTHING YOU CAN DO — Syndication 1971

Stunt show. Original host: Gene Wood.

ARE YOU POSITIVE? — NBC 1952

A panel of sportswriters tried to guess the identities of sports heroes from film negatives and childhood photos. It was also called BILL STERN'S SPORTS QUIZ. Original host: Bill Stern.

ARMCHAIR DETECTIVE — CBS 1949

Crimes were reenacted for the studio audience, which then attempted to solve them. Original host: John Milton Kennedy.

AUCTION-AIRE — ABC 1949

An actual auctioneer led the bidding as viewers competed for merchandise. Original host: Jack Gregson.

B

THE BABY GAME — ABC 1949

Three couples competed to see who knew the most about child behavior. Original host: Richard Hayes.

BACK THAT FACT — ABC 1953

Contestants from the studio audience were encouraged to answer questions about their childhoods, jobs, etc. The gimmick was that at some point the announcer would interrupt and ask them to "back that fact." If they could convince a panel from the audience that they were telling the truth they won a prize. Original host: Joey Adams.

BAFFLE — NBC 1973

Celebrity word game (See: P.D.Q.) Original host: Dick Enberg.

BALANCE YOUR BUDGET — CBS 1952

The woman of the house answered questions about home finance. Original host: Bert Parks.

BANK ON THE STARS — CBS 1953; NBC 1954

Contestant teams were shown clips from movies and quizzed about them. Bonus round involved hearing a scene but not seeing it. Original host: Bill Cullen.

BARGAIN HUNTERS — ABC 1987

Bargain basement THE PRICE IS RIGHT. Original host: Peter Tomarken.

BATTLESTARS — NBC 1981

Six celebs sat in a Hollywood triangle instead of a Hollywood square in this HOLLYWOOD SQUARES copycat. Original host: Alex Trebek.

BEACH CLASH — Syndication 1995

AMERICAN GLADIATORS knockoff set on the surf in sunny California. The outdoor setting gives plenty of opportunities to show off tanned, hardbodies in skimpy clothes.

BEAT THE CLOCK* — CBS 1950

The one and only. Classic stunt show with a time limit. Original host: Bud Collyer.

BEAT THE ODDS — Syndication 1969

The contestants spun an alphabet wheel to get two letters from which they had to make a word. For instance: C and R could make CAR. Original host: Johnny Gilbert.

BEDTIME STORIES — Syndication 1979

Silly Q & A with a sexual edge hosted by two L.A. radio personalities. Original Hosts: Al Lohman and Roger Barkley.

THE BETTER SEX — ABC 1977

Teams of men and women competed against each other in a Q & A battle of the sexes. Original hosts: Bill Anderson and Sara Purcell.

BID 'N 'BUY — CBS 1958

One of the many bid-for-merchandise PRICE IS RIGHT copies. Original host: Bert Parks.

THE BIG GAME — NBC 1958

Contestants went to the jungle via a game board to collect opponents' animals by answering questions about them and then "shooting them" to add them to their collection. Original host: Tom Kennedy.

THE BIG PAYOFF *— NBC 1952

Male viewers became contestants on this Q & A by writing in about how wonderful their spouses were. Once selected, the guys had to answer questions to reap big prizes for their loved one. Original host: Randy Merriman.

THE BIG SHOWDOWN — ABC 1974

Q & A with a dice role for the bonus round that determined cash and prizes. Original host: Jim Peck.

THE BIG SURPRISE* — NBC 1955

Big money intelligence tester with cash prizes of $100 to $100,000 for ten progressively difficult questions. Original host: Jack Barry (later: Mike Wallace.)

BILL STERN'S SPORTS QUIZ

The other title for ARE YOU POSITIVE?

BLADE WARRIORS — Syndication 1995

Young adults on rollerblades compete on an obstacle course. It looks dangerous and it is.

BLANK CHECK — NBC 1975

Five players competed in tough Q & A for the right to a "blank check." Original host: Art James.

BLANKETY BLANKS — ABC 1975

The final round in this Q & A was a riddle with a missing word. Original host: Bill Cullen.

BLIND DATE — ABC 1949

The original "DATING GAME." Six college guys separated by a wall from a gorgeous model tried to convince her to go out with them by the way they answered her questions over a telephone hookup. During the Korean War servicemen subbed for the frat crowd. Original host: Arlene Francis.

BLOCKBUSTERS — NBC 1980

Q & A that used a letter to substitute for the necessary word. "What famous C is the host of a talk show?" Johnny Carson. Original host: Bill Cullen.

BODY LANGUAGE — CBS 1984

Team charades. Original host: Tom Kennedy.

BORN LUCKY — Syndication 1991

Set on location in a shopping mall, contestants were picked from a throng of shoppers and offered the chance to win mall money, which they had to spend on site.

BRAINS AND BRAWN — NBC 1958

As the name suggests, a contest between jocks and eggheads who were questioned about each other's area of expertise. Original Hosts: Jack Lescoulie (brawn) Fred Davis (brains).

Break The Bank* — ABC 1948

Category Q & A with increasing amounts of money as the questions got more difficult. Original host: Bert Parks.

Break The $250,000 Bank — ABC 1956

Big-money version of Break The Bank. Original host: Bert Parks

Broadway to Hollywood Headline Clues — Dumont 1949

The most important part of this early magazine show was a call-in Q & A in which the viewers at home answered questions about current events for cash and prizes. Original host: George Putnam.

Bruce Forsyth's Hot Streak — ABC 1986

A very short-lived Family Feud knockoff. The hook was that the host was a big deal in the Australian game show circuit. Original host: Bruce Forsyth.

Bullseye — Syndication 1980

A wheel game in which the spin decided the difficulty and value of the questions. Original host: Jim Lange.

Did You Know That...

Ed McMahon is 6'4" tall.

C

CALL MY BLUFF — NBC 1965

Based on the parlor game called "Dictionary," this contest required contestants to figure out which definition of a specific word was correct and which ones were made up by the panel. Original host: Bill Leyden.

CAMOUFLAGE — ABC 1961

A portion of an illustration was shown to the players. The more correct answers, the more of the illustration was revealed until someone guessed what it was. Original host: Tom Campbell.

CAN DO — NBC 1956

A panel of contestants guessed whether a celebrity guest would be able to perform a stunt. Original host: Robert Aida.

CAN YOU TOP THIS — ABC 1950

Comedians competed with each other for the funniest joke. The audience decided who won by their response on the laugh meter. Original host: Ward Wilson.

CARD SHARKS — NBC 1978

A complicated guessing/gambling game in which the contestant who predicted the results of an opinion poll would compete in a card-turning contest attempting to guess whether the next card would be higher or lower. Original host: Jim Perry.

CASH AND CARRY* — DUMONT 1946

Set in a supermarket, CASH AND CARRY was the first game show carried on a national network. Contestants roamed the aisles picking products tagged with questions worth varying amounts of cash. There was also a stunt section. Original host: Dennis James.

Catch Phrase — Syndication 1985

A picture puzzle (rebus) hid a phrase. Guess the phrase and win. Original host: Art James.

Celebrity Charades — Syndication 1979

A team charades game unique because it was hosted by a ventriloquist and his dummy. Hosts: Jay Johnson and Squeaky.

The Celebrity Game — CBS 1964

Contestants predicted how a panel of nine celebrities would vote on a specific issue. The Celebrity Game was the basis for The Hollywood Squares. Original host: Carl Reiner.

Celebrity Sweepstakes — NBC 1974

Another Hollywood Squares copy in which contestants would guess which of the celebrity panel would correctly answer a question. Original host: Jim McKrell.

Celebrity Time — CBS 1946

Celebrities solved riddles. Original host: Conrad Nagel.

Chain Letter — NBC 1966

Teams were given a topic for which they had to come up with appropriate words. Original host: Jan Murray.

Chance For Romance — ABC 1958

Another early Dating Game. The show is notable for being hosted by a former newscaster. Original host: John Cameron Swayze.

The Charade Quiz — Dumont 1947

Viewers suggested charades which a group of actors performed for a panel. The viewer got $15 if the panel couldn't guess the answer. Original host: Bill Slater.

CHARGE ACCOUNT — NBC 1960

A Scrabble-type crossword game in which contestants who made the most words out of their sixteen letters could buy prizes in the Video Store. Original host: Jan Murray.

THE CHEAP SHOW — Syndication 1978

Like TRUTH OR CONSEQUENCES, THE CHEAP SHOW provided bizarre penalties for contestants who were unable to do silly stunts. The prizes for success were chosen from a wheel powered by a rat. You gotta love it. Original host: Dick Martin.

CHILD'S PLAY — CBS 1982

Children were asked questions and their answers were videotaped. Contestants listened to the answers and had to decide what the youngsters were talking about. Original host: Bill Cullen.

CHOOSE UP SIDES — NBC 1956

Stunt format for children. Original host: Gene Rayburn.

CLASSIC CONCENTRATION — NBC 1987

See CONCENTRATION. Original host: Alex Trebek.

COME CLOSER — ABC 1954

Q & A with ventriloquist Jimmy Nelson whose most famous dummy was Farfel the Dog.

CONCENTRATION* — NBC 1958

A rebus of thirty squares was presented to contestants who attempted to match similar items by revealing two squares at a time. The trick was to remember which squares held matching prizes or cash or penalties because the squares were rehidden if a match wasn't made. Original host: Jack Barry.

CRIME TIME — CBS 1960

A tribute to the criminal element—sort of. Contestants with dubious pasts traded recipes, tried to explain away their crimes, and competed in events like safecracking against the clock. Original host: Anonymous.

CROSS-WITS* — Syndication 1975

Another classic. Solve the crossword puzzle using two teams composed of two celebrities and a contestant each, and win a chance to advance to the Crossfire round where the object was to fill in ten words in 60 seconds. The grand prize was a trip to an exotic foreign city like Paris, France. Original host: Jack Clark.

D

THE DATING GAME* — ABC 1965

The one and only. A bachelorette interviewed three bachelors and chose one for a date. Original host: Jim Lange.

DEALER'S CHOICE — Syndication 1973

Casino-type card games for prizes. Vegas style. The show was trash and glitz broadcast from the Tropicana. Original host: Bob Hastings.

THE DIAMOND HEAD GAME — Syndication 1975

The exotic locale, a Hawaiian beach, and a finale that took place in a glass cage, and involved cash prizes and a wind machine weren't enough to keep this Q & A going. Original host: Bob Eubanks.

DO YOU KNOW? — CBS 1963

English literature for children. Original host: Bob Maxwell.

DO YOU TRUST YOUR WIFE?* — CBS 1956

Edgar Bergen and his collection of dummies questioned and poked fun at contestants who had to determine whether or not their spouses would be able to answer certain questions. Hosts: Edgar Bergen and his dummies: Charlie McCarthy, Mortimer Snerd, and Effie Klinker.

DOCTOR I.Q. — ABC 1953

Q & A format where assistants roamed the auditorium with microphones selecting participants, calling "Doctor, I have a lady in the second row." The doctor would then ask a question and if he received the correct answer would award silver dollars calling "Give the lady in the second row ten silver dollars!" The show was a huge success on radio before it moved to television. The doctor: Jay Owen.

DOLLAR A SECOND* — DUMONT 1953

Another classic. Participants won a dollar for each second they could stay on the show. Original host: Jan Murray.

THE $1.98 BEAUTY CONTEST — Syndication 1978

Chuck Barris insanity at its best. Weird, wacky, strange, and sometimes sexy contestants hit the runway in front of a panel of celebrities who voted for the "winner." Original host: Rip Taylor.

DOTTO — NBC 1958

Connect the dots, recognize the celebrity caricature, and win the prize. DOTTO was the first show to fall during the rigging scandals of the late 50s.
Original host: Jack Narz.

Double Dare — CBS 1976

Contestants were given clues that added up to a specific answer. The first one to guess correctly could collect the prize or dare the opponent to guess correctly using more clues. If the opponent couldn't guess, the winner got more money. Original host: Alex Trebek.

Double Dare — Nickelodeon 1986

This particular DOUBLE DARE was an all children's stunt format full of water hoses, colored slime, eggs, and lots of gooey fun. The show went to FOX in 1988, adding parents to the mix. It's the first game show that originated on cable before moving to syndication as FAMILY DOUBLE DARE. Original host: Marc Summers.

Double Exposure — CBS 1961

The face of a famous person was hidden in a jigsaw puzzle. Original host: Steve Dunne.

Double or Nothing — CBS 1952

A radio transplant Q & A that allowed a contestant to go double or nothing on a fifth question after answering four correctly. Original host: Bert Parks.

Double Talk — ABC 1986

Teams of contestants had to translate slang. Original host: Henry Polic, II.

Dough Re Mi — NBC 1958

Three contestants competed to guess the name of a song after hearing just three notes. Original host: Gene Rayburn.

Down You Go* — CBS 1951

Classic of the celebrity panel show genre based on Hangman. The panelists made it great. Original host: Dr. Bergen Evans.

Draw Me A Laugh — ABC 1949

A panel of cartoonists drew cartoons based on viewer ideas. One got the sketch, the other just the caption. The audience decided which was funnier. Original host: Walter Hurley.

Draw To Win — CBS 1952

Celebrities identified people, places and things from quick sketches. Original host: Henry Morgan.

Dream Girl of '67 — ABC 1966

A marginally serious Chuck Barris beauty pageant. Original host: Dick Stewart.

Dream House — ABC 1968

Couples answered a series of questions for which they received rooms of furniture. If they were able to stay on long enough to win four rounds in a row, they also got a dream house, which could be anything from a trailer to a private island off the coast of Maine. Original host: Mike Darrow.

Droodles — NBC 1954

A comedy quiz which required celebrities to guess the meaning or title of nonsense drawings submitted by viewers or drawn by the host, who had written a best-selling book called *Droodles* that spawned the series. Original host: Roger Price.

Did You Know That...

After James Dean (stunt tester for BEAT THE CLOCK) became a star he returned again and again to the studio in New York to visit friends and eat the commissary's rice pudding, which he claimed was his favorite.

E

Earn Your Vacation — CBS 1954

If Johnny liked your vacation fantasy, he would invite you onstage for more questions and the chance to actually fulfill it. Original host: Johnny Carson.

E.S.P. — ABC 1958

Audience members were tested by a team of psychologists for extra sensory potential, then brought on the show to test their skills in a Q & A format. It was a disaster and the format was replaced after only three shows with a lame attempt at drama called *Tales of E.S.P.* Original host: Vincent Price.

Every Second Counts — Syndication 1984

After winning the first round of Q & A the contestants walked up a large staircase answering questions as they went. Of course, there was a time limit, but if you got to the top, you won a car. Original host: Bill Rafferty.

Everybody's Talking — ABC 1967

Players listened to clips of unedited conversations, and tried to guess what the people were talking about. Original host: Lloyd Thaxton.

Everything's Relative — Syndication 1965

Two family teams competed to predict whether one of their family members could answer a question or accomplish a simple task. Original host: Jim Hutton.

Eye Guess — NBC 1966

A real memory test. For eight seconds players were shown a board with eight answers. Then they were read the questions. The first to get seven correct won the game. Original host: Bill Cullen.

F

THE FACE IS FAMILIAR — CBS 1966

Teams competed to guess the identity of a famous person from a scrambled photograph. Original host: Jack Whitaker.

FACE THE FACTS — CBS 1961

Players watched a criminal case until just before the conclusion and tried to guess how it all turned out. Original host: Red Rowe.

FACE THE MUSIC — Syndication 1980

NAME THAT TUNE again but hosted by ex-Tarzan, Ron Ely.

FAMILY DOUBLE DARE — FOX 1988

Stunt show spin-off from Nickelodeon's DOUBLE DARE that probably wins the prize for messiest ever. Teams of families, two parents and two children each, sprayed seltzer, threw eggs, sloshed through syrup and other sticky crud for cash and prizes. The winning team ran an obstacle course for the big bucks. Original host: Marc Summers.

FAMILY FEUD* — ABC 1976

To win prizes and money teams of families guessed at the results of audience polls. Original host: Richard Dawson.

FAMILY GAME —ABC 1967

Yet another spin-off of THE NEWLYWED GAME. This time the teams were composed of three all-American families including Mom, Dad, and two children. The children had to predict how their parents would answer certain questions. Original host: Bob Barker.

G

GAMBIT — CBS 1972

Blackjack game show style. As cards were dealt by the lovely Elaine Stewart, the contestants had to answer questions to move ahead without going over 21. GAMBIT ended its run broadcasting from Las Vegas. Original host: Wink Martindale.

GAMBLE ON LOVE — DUMONT 1954

A wheel of fortune decided the questions to be asked of three young couples. Hostess: Denise Darcel.

THE GAME GAME — Syndication 1969

Players guessed how a celeb had responded to a question. Original host: Jim McKrell.

THE G.E. COLLEGE BOWL* — CBS 1959

Teams of students representing their college competed for scholarships and the honor of returning until they were unseated. Original host: Allen Ludden.

G.E. GUEST HOUSE — CBS 1951

A panel of celebrities, consisting of a critic, a writer, a performer, and a producer tested their knowledge of the entertainment business. Original host: Oscar Levant.

THE GENERATION GAP — ABC 1969

A team of adults mixed it up with a team of teenagers. The adults had to know about current fads and the teens were questioned about past cultural icons. Original host: Dennis Whaley.

GET THE MESSAGE — ABC 1954

A PASSWORD knockoff using two-word clues instead of one. Original host: Frank Buxton.

GHOST — NBC 1952

The players were given the number of letters in a word and had to fill in and guess the word without adding the last letter. Based on the children's game of the same name. Original host: Dr. Bergen Evans.

GIANT STEP — CBS 1956

High school students went head to head answering difficult questions to win a free college education. Original host: Bert Parks.

THE GIRL IN MY LIFE — ABC 1973

Special women were rewarded by the men in their lives for the good deeds they had performed. Original host: Fred Holliday.

GIVE AND TAKE — CBS 1952

Standard studio audience Q & A. Original host: Bill Cullen.

GIVE-N-TAKE — CBS 1975

Four women answered questions and collected prizes. The trick was not to go over a total retail prize value of $4,900. Once they reached $5,000 anything they had won was returned to the Give-N-Take store. Original host: Jim Lange.

GLADIATORS 2000 — Syndication 1995

A children's version of the hard-as-nails game show with an educational bent. Wearing helmets and pads, the wee ones run around collecting giant fruits and vegetables or learning how to brush their teeth with mammoth toothbrushes.

GLAMOUR GIRL — NBC 1953

Four women from the studio audience competed in a beauty contest and the audience picked the winner. Original host: Harry Babbitt.

Go! — NBC 1983

The object of this team game was to construct a question one word at a time and thereby guess the answer. Original host: Kevin O'Connell.

Go Lucky — CBS 1951

Charades. Original host: Jan Murray.

The Gong Show* — NBC 1976

A wacky and bizarre entry that fits very loosely into the stunt-show category. Contestants performed in a talent show and hoped that the panel wouldn't gong them off the stage before they finished. Original host: Gary Owens.

The Greatest Man On Earth — ABC 1952

Five guys from the studio audience answered questions and performed stunts to gain the title of Greatest Man on Earth. Original host: Ted Brown.

Guess Again — CBS 1951

Contestants watched a skit and then answered questions about it. Original host: Mike Wallace.

Guess What Happened? — NBC 1952

Contestants who had recently been in the news appeared on the show. The panel tried to figure out the story. Original host: John Cameron Swayze.

The Guinness Game — Syndication 1979

The contestants guessed whether a person who already had a record in the *Guinness Book of World Records* could break it. Original host: Don Galloway.

H

HAGGIS BAGGIS — NBC 1958

A recognize-the-celebrity-as-pieces-of-a-puzzle-are-revealed game. The winner had a choice of Haggis, which were expensive trifles, or Baggis which were more useful stuff. Original host: Art Linkletter.

HAVE A HEART — DUMONT 1955

The most altruistic Q & A in game show history because the winners gave their loot to charities. Original host: John Reed King

HE SAID, SHE SAID — Syndication 1969

A celebrity version of the NEWLYWED format with four famous couples deciding how their spouses would respond to various questions. Original host: Joe Garagiola.

HEADLINE CHASERS — Syndication 1985

A current-events Q & A using actual newspaper headlines as sources of information. Original host: Wink Martindale.

HIGH FINANCE — CBS 1956

Players were given a bankroll which they "invested" to win cash and prizes. Original host: Dennis James.

HIGH-LOW — NBC 1956

Questions were broken into sections and players got increasing amounts of cash the more parts they were able to answer. Played as a Hi-Lo poker game. Original host: Jack Barry.

HIGH ROLLERS* — NBC 1974

After a Q & A session winners got the chance to roll dice for bonus prizes. Original host: Alex Trebek.

HIT MAN — NBC 1983

Three against one. A Q & A in which challengers tried to unseat the current winner. Original host: Peter Tomarken.

HOLD IT PLEASE — CBS 1949

A troupe of performers acted out answers to questions on current events. The players competed for a $1,000 jackpot and the right to be an assistant emcee until they were dethroned. Fates went on to produce WHAT'S MY LINE?, I'VE GOT A SECRET, and TO TELL THE TRUTH. Original host: Gil Fates.

HOLD THAT NOTE — NBC 1957

The gimmick on this musical quiz was that the fewer notes it took to guess the name, the more money for the contestant. Original host: Bert Parks.

HOLLYWOOD CONNECTION — Syndication 1977

Predict the celebrity answer. Original host: Jim Lange.

THE HOLLYWOOD SQUARES* — NBC 1966

Tic-Tac-Toe with nine celebrities sitting inside a giant board. The celebrity answerd a question to earn an X or an O, and the contestant guessed if the answer was right, wrong , or a bluff. Original host: Peter Marshall.

HOLLYWOOD'S TALKING — CBS 1973

Clips of celebrities talking were shown to a contestant who had to guess what the celeb was talking about. Original host: Geoff Edwards.

THE HONEYMOON GAME — Syndication 1971

Three couples competed for a special honeymoon getaway. Original host: Jim McKrell.

HOT POTATO — NBC 1984

Teams of three competed to guess the results of a poll. Original host: Bill Cullen.

Hot Seat — ABC 1976

The husband was asked the questions. The wife guessed how he would answer. The husband was given a lie-detector test to verify the truth. Wow. Original host: Jim Peck.

How Do You Rate? — CBS 1958

A serious quiz involving weighty issues such as logic and math. Original host: Tom Reddy.

How's Your Mother-In-Law? — ABC 1967

Celebrity judges decided which player had the best mother-in-law based on how the husband or wife pitched her. Original host: Wink Martindale.

I

I'll Bet — NBC 1965

Husbands placed bets on whether their wives would be able to answer a general-knowledge question. Original host: Jack Narz.

I'll Buy That — CBS 1953

Merchandise and prizes were covered by black cloths. The contestants, chosen from the studio audience, were given clues by the host. When they guessed the identity of a prize, it was theirs if they could guess the cost. Original host: Mike Wallace.

I'm Telling — NBC 1987

A chance for brothers and sisters to get back at each other in THE NEWLYWED GAME format.

Infatuation — Syndication 1992

One of the guests had a secret crush on the other one for some time. The secret is revealed on the air and the couple discuss it in front of a few million people. Original host: Bob Eubanks.

Information Please — CBS 1952

Viewers sent in tough questions to be answered by a literate and well-read panel. Viewers who stumped the panel were awarded a gift certificate good for books or magazines. Though only a summer replacement for one season on television, this quality show had a long and successful run on radio. Original host: Clifton Fadiman.

It Could Be You — NBC 1956

This Is Your Life meets Truth or Consequences. Members of the studio audience were chosen and reunited with friends or relatives and then performed stunts for prizes. Original host: Bill Leyden.

It Pays To Be Ignorant — CBS 1949

Simple questions equaled silly, wacky, and hilarious answers on this show in which the point was to elicit as much zaniness as possible from a panel of comics. The contestant struggled amidst the madness to get in the right answer. Original host: "Professor" Tom Howard.

It Pays To Be Married — CBS 1955

More real-life as couples bared their souls about the problems they had overcome in their marriages and answered questions for money. Original host: Bill Goodwin.

It Pays To Be Stupid — Syndication 1973

An even more stupid spinoff of the 1949 It Pays To Be Ignorant. Original host: Joe Flynn.

It Takes Two — NBC 1969

Three celebrity couples, one member of the studio audience. The contestant picked which couple would be most likely to correctly answer the question. Original host: Vin Scully.

Did You Know That...

Barbara Walters was a prize model on an early New York game show: NBC's ASK THE CAMERA, with host Sandy Becker.

IT'S ABOUT TIME — ABC 1954

A history quiz using scrambled hints to stump the panel. Original host: Dr. Bergen Evans.

IT'S ANYBODY'S GUESS — NBC 1977

Players predicted audience response to studio polls. Original host: Monty Hall.

IT'S NEWS TO ME — CBS 1951

Current-events questions posed to a panel by a newscaster. Original host: Walter Cronkite.

IT'S YOUR BET — Syndication 1969

Update of I'LL BET with celebrities. The show had a four-year run. Original host: Hal March.

I'VE GOT A SECRET* — CBS 1952

The classic. A contestant had a secret. It was the job of the panel to figure out what it was. Original host: Garry Moore.

I'VE GOT NEWS FOR YOU — NBC 1952

Current events with members of the studio audience. Original host: Jack Paar.

J

Jackpot — NBC 1974

The largest assemblage of contestants in gamedom. Eight teams, sixteen players in all. A riddle game in which the object was to remain in the Winner's Circle by guessing the answer. Original host: Geoff Edwards.

Jackpot Bowling Starring Milton Berle — NBC 1961

Bowlers competed for prizes and cash with bonuses for special combinations. Berle, who replaced sportscasters Mel Allen and Bud Palmer and got his name added to the show title, provided the comedy between matches. Right. Original host: Milton Berle.

Jeopardy!* — NBC 1964

The perennial favorite and still going strong. Players get the answers on a big category board and have to give the questions. Original host: Art Fleming.

Joe Garagiola's Memory Game — NBC 1971

Five women, $50, five questions. Twenty seconds to study them. Hand them back to the host. The host asks the questions. Right answers are worth $5, wrong answers cost $5 and give the next contestant a chance to answer. Complicated? Yes. Too complicated. Yes. Original host: Take a guess.

The Joker's Wild — CBS 1972

70s glitz. The main set piece was a giant slot machine which contestants used to win bonuses for correct answers. Original host: Jack Barry.

Joker! Joker! Joker! — Syndication 1979

Son of The Joker's Wild. Original host: Jack Barry.

THE JOKE'S ON US — Syndication 1983

A panel of comics came up with punch lines to jokes submitted by viewers. One of the punchlines was right. The players had to guess which one. Original host: Monty Hall.

JUDGE FOR YOURSELF — NBC 1953

Talent contest in which members of the audience competed with a panel of professional talent judgers to decide which of the acts presented were good. If the audience members picked the same acts as the pros, they won prizes and cash. Original host: Fred Allen.

JUST MEN — NBC 1983

Five men talking about their lives for cash and prizes. Original host: Betty White.

JUVENILE JURY* — NBC 1947

A panel of children were presented with viewer-submitted problems or questions and the "Juvenile Jury" was asked to mediate or solve them. The results were always entertaining and often hilarious. Original host: Jack Barry.

K

KAY KYSER'S KOLLEGE OF MUSICAL KNOWLEDGE* — NBC 1949

A dispute with the producers led to an early demise for this wacky musical Q & A in which a troupe of actors and singers performed musical questions. Original host: Big-band leader, Kay Kyser.

KEEP IT IN THE FAMILY — ABC 1957

Family groups competed to answer several connected questions at once. A presager of FAMILY FEUD. Original host: Bill Nimmo.

Keep Talking — CBS 1958

The first contestant was given a secret phrase. His or her job was to weave it into a story. The others had to guess what the phrase was. Original host: Monty Hall.

Knockout — NBC 1977

An object-association game in which players earned letters to spell the word KNOCKOUT by looking at groups of things and deciding which didn't belong. Original host: Arte Johnson.

The Krypton Factor — ABC 1981

Contestants performed super stunts and answered questions to win cash and prizes. Original host: Dick Clark.

L

Ladies Be Seated — ABC 1949

Q & A plus parlor games with penalties took this Chicago-based local to the network for a short run. Original host: Tom Moore.

Las Vegas Gambit — NBC 1980

The hook for this new version of the blackjack game GAMBIT was that it was shot at the Tropicana in Vegas. Original host: Wink Martindale.

Laugh Line — NBC 1959

The viewing audience submitted ideas for silent skits complete with punch lines that were performed by a team of comic actors which sometimes included the then comedy team of Mike Nichols and Elaine May. A panel of celebs had to guess a punch line of their own, based on what they saw. The audience judged which was funnier, and if it picked the viewer's, the viewer won a prize. Original host: Dick Van Dyke.

LEGENDS OF THE HIDDEN TEMPLE — NICKELODEON 1995

Once again the kids get dressed up in pads and helmets and go on fantasy hunts for various treasures in exotic and creative enviroments. A safe but "live" Indiana Jones. Semi-host: A big stone face that sounded like, but wasn't, James Earl Jones.

LET'S MAKE A DEAL* — NBC 1963

Contestants put on wacky costumes and made fools of themselves to get a chance to trade their own stuff for prizes that they could see or prizes that were hidden behind the famous doors. One of the great ones. Original host: Monty Hall.

LET'S PLAY POST OFFICE — NBC 1965

The players listened to fictitious letters written in the style of famous people. If they guessed the correct writer, they won. Original host: Don Morrow.

LET'S SEE — ABC 1955

Maybe the first infomercial ever broadcast, this quiz show asked panelists to figure out where a contestant had been in Atlantic City by asking indirect questions. It was sponsored (no kidding) by the Atlantic City Chamber of Commerce. Original host: John Reed King.

LETTERS TO LAUGH-IN — NBC 1969

Spinning off and cashing in on the phenomenal success of *Laugh-In*, viewer-submitted items were read aloud to the audience which judged entries for their humor. Original host: Gary Owens.

LIAR'S CLUB — Syndication 1969

Only Rod Serling could be the original host of this one. Panelists were shown strange objects and asked to come up with explanations of what they were and how to use them. Contestants had to decide which panelist was telling the truth and bet their stake accordingly. The show appeared off and on for several years. Original host: Rod Serling.

LIE DETECTOR — CBS 1983

Newsworthy types, such as Ronald Reagan's hairdresser, were grilled to get them to tell all, and then they were given a polygraph test. Original host: F. Lee Bailey.

LIFE BEGINS AT EIGHTY* — NBC 1950

The appeal of this spin-off of JUVENILE JURY is evident in the fact that it ran for over six years. A panel of wise and clever gray hairs answered questions and got a chance to give life the perspective of years. Original host: Jack Barry.

LIFE WITH LINKLETTER — ABC 1950

The night time version of *House Party.* The appeal, as always, was the host. Original host: Art Linkletter.

LIP SERVICE — MTV 1992

Rock 'n Roll version of BEAT THE CLOCK and NAME THAT TUNE. The object: guess whose lips were in the video close-up. Original host: Dr. Joyce Brothers.

LOVE CONNECTION — Syndication 1983

Couples were paired up by video and went out on a date. They appeared on the show to relate the gory details and decide if they would go out again. Original host: Chuck Wollery.

THE LOVE EXPERTS — Syndication 1978

Advice on love problems was given by a celebrity panel. The best problem won a prize. Original host: Bill Cullen.

LUCKY PARTNERS — NBC 1958

Contestants tried to match serial numbers on dollar bills.
Original host: Carl Cordell.

M

MADE IN AMERICA — CBS 1964

Self-made millionnaires were questioned by a panel whose job
it was to guess how they made their pile. Original host: Bob
Maxwell.

THE MAGNIFICENT MARBLE MACHINE — NBC 1975

A giant pinball machine, two teams. Glitz and machinery for
prizes. Original host: Art James.

MAJORITY RULES — ABC 1949

Three contestants answered a question and the right answer
was determined by the majority opinion. Mike Wallace, then
known as Myron, was a later host of the Chicago-based show.
Original host: Ed Prentiss.

MAKE A FACE — ABC 1961

Players guessed the identity of a celebrity by unscrambling a
jumbled photo. Original host: Bob Clayton.

MAKE ME LAUGH — ABC 1958

A comic tried to make a contestant break up. The contestants
won if they could keep a straight face. Original host: Robert Q.
Lewis.

MAKE THE CONNECTION — NBC 1955

Panelists guessed how contestants knew each other. Original
host: Jim McKay.

MASQUERADE PARTY* — NBC 1952

One of the biggies in gameshowdom. Celebrities disguised themselves, and the contestants had to guess their identity. Original host: Bud Collyer.

THE MATCH GAME* — NBC 1962

Celebrities answered questions or filled in the blanks in a sentence. Contestants tried to match them. A major show in the game world. Original host: Gene Rayburn.

THE MATCH GAME / HOLLYWOOD SQUARES HOUR — NBC 1983

Two successful shows combined for reasons known only to the producers. Original host: Gene Rayburn.

MATCHES 'N' MATES — ABC 1967

Married couples matched answers with questions. Original host: Art James.

MINDREADERS — NBC 1979

Contestants predicted how panelists would answer a question. Original host: Dick Martin.

MISSING LINKS — NBC 1963

Contestants listened to a story with missing information. They picked a celebrity they felt would do the best job of filling in the blanks. Original host: Ed McMahon.

MISSUS GOES A-SHOPPING — CBS 1944 (LOCAL), 1947 (NATIONAL)

A local New York show that vies with CASH AND CARRY for first of a genre, (first network game show). This shopping for prizes went national in early 1947, but CASH AND CARRY was probably on as early as 1946. Original host: John Reed King.

MONEY MAKERS — Syndication 1969

Bingo for the studio and home audience. Original host: Jim Perry.

MONEY MAZE — ABC 1974

The wacked out 70s at their best. If the contestant was able to answer the question correctly, they had to run through a maze to collect their money. Original host: Nick Clooney.

MONOPOLY — ABC 1990

The great board game of the Depression brought to high-tech reality on the tube. Three contestants competed on a huge rendition of the famous setup. Original host: Michael Reilly.

MOTHER'S DAY — ABC 1958

Moms answered questions about problems and issues around the home. The winner, as judged by the audience, became Mother of the Day. The title came with some merchandise. Original host: Dick Van Dyke.

THE MOVIE GAME — Syndication 1969

Stars answered questions about films. Amy Archerd, a *Variety* columnist, was on hand to mediate. Original host: Sonny Fox.

MOVIELAND QUIZ — ABC 1948

In front of a set that depicted a movie theater complete with ticket taker, the host asked contestants to guess stars and titles of films from selected clips. Original host: Arthur Q. Bryan.

MUSIC BINGO — NBC 1958

Snatches of a tune were played, contestants pushed a buzzer when they could guess the name. Correct answers got the players a sharp or a flat on the bingo board. They continued guessing and filling in the board until someone got a complete row and won the game. Original host: Johnny Gilbert.

MUSICAL CHAIRS — NBC 1955

Why a show that quizzed panelists Mel Blanc, Johnny Mercer, and Bobby Troup on a broad range of question about music and asked them to perform in the style of famous performers was called MUSICAL CHAIRS is anybody's guess. Original host: Bill Leyden.

MUSICAL CHAIRS — CBS 1975

More to the point. More like the parlor game, this effort asked contestants to guess a tune and if they were wrong, they lost their chair. Original host: Adam Wade.

N

THE NAME DROPPERS — NBC 1969

The name dropper gave hints about his or her relationship to a celebrity. The contestant had to guess who they were talking about. Original co-hosts: Al Lohman and Roger Barkley (A pair of L.A. DJ's).

NAME THAT TUNE *— NBC 1953

One of the granddaddies of the musical guessing games and probably the longest running. Original host: Red Benson (although Bill Cullen was the most famous).

THE NAME'S THE SAME* — ABC 1951

Regular people who happened to share the same name as a celebrity or figure from history came on the show to stump the panel. Panelists had to figure out with whom the contestants shared a famous moniker. Original host: Robert Q. Lewis..

NEIGHBORS — ABC 1975

Real neighbors shared a little gossip with the studio audience and won prizes for the best receipe. Original host: Regis Philbin.

THE NEW PRICE IS RIGHT — CBS 1986

What else is there to say? Original host: Bob Barker.

THE NEW SUPERMARKET SWEEP — LIFETIME 1994

The same show as SUPERMARKET SWEEP some years later with a riddle-driven treasure hunt for the winners at the end.

THE NEWLYWED GAME* — ABC 1966

Couples were separately asked the same set of questions. Then each predicted how the other would answer. Original host: Bob Eubanks.

NIGHT GAMES — SYNDICATION 1991

Late night, more sexually explicit version of the Dating Game. Contestants performed "sensual foot massages" and the like to win dinner for two at a swank Los Angeles eatery. Big winners got a romantic weekend in a romantic place.
Original host: Jeff Marder

NOW YOU SEE IT — CBS 1974

A maze game in two dimensions. Contestants looked for hidden answers. Original host: Jack Narz.

NUMBER PLEASE — ABC 1961

A call-in Hangman game in which the viewers answered questions to fill in the board. Original host: Bud Collyer.

O

THE OBJECT IS — ABC 1963

Celebs and contestants worked to identify the names of famous people. Original host: Dick Clark.

OH, MY WORD — Syndication 1966

Another dictionary game in which celebrity panelists tried to guess the meaning of obscure and strange words. Original host: Jim Lange.

ON YOUR ACCOUNT — NBC 1953

A sob-story spin-off in which a panel rated the saddest tale of woe and awarded cash to the most deserving. Original host: Eddie Albert.

ON YOUR WAY — DUMONT 1953

If your particular talent made you the winner, you were sent to the destination of your choice. Original host: Bud Collyer.

ONE HUNDRED GRAND — ABC 1963

Contestants challenged the panel of experts to quiz them in their specific field of knowledge. If they won, they answered questions submitted by viewers. The first large dollar show after the scandals. Nobody won. Original host: Jack Clark.

THE $100,000 BIG SURPRISE — NBC 1956

A higher-dollar version of THE BIG SURPRISE. Original host: Mike Wallace.

THE $100,000 NAME THAT TUNE — Syndication 1974

Same tune, more money. Original host: Tom Kennedy.

THE $128,000 QUESTION — Syndication 1976

Even big dough couldn't make this update of THE $64,000 QUESTION fly. Original host: Mike Darrow.

ONE IN A MILLION — ABC 1967

Everyone on the panel shared a secret. Contestants had to figure it out. Original host: Danny O'Neil.

The One Million Dollar Chance Of A Lifetime — Syndication 1986

Top dollar amount ever offered in a game show. Contestants had to solve puzzles three days in a row. Original host: Jim Lange.

One Minute Please — DUMONT 1954

A panel of zanies, including the likes of Ernie Kovacs and Hermione Gingold, were given subjects such as *Breeding Guppies* or *Why I Ride Sidesaddle* and competed for who could say the most nonsense about the ridiculous subject in one minute. Original host: John K. M. McCaffery.

P

Pantomime Quiz* — CBS 1949

The top of the line in the charades genre. Celebrity teams competed in lively and exciting competitions with material sent in by viewers. Original host: Mike Stokey.

The Parent Game — Syndication 1972

The Newlywed Game for three sets of young parents. They tried to match their answers with those of an expert on child care. The most matches won. Original host: Clark Race.

Party Line — NBC 1947

A call-in Q & A with questions illustrated with drawings or film clips. Viewers sent in cards with phone numbers and were called at random. If they were home and were right, they won $5 and a box of goodies from sponsor Bristol Myers. Original host: Bert Parks.

PASS THE BUCK — CBS 1978

If you couldn't answer the question, you were sent to the "bull pen" where you waited to return if another contestant couldn't answer the question. The idea was to eliminate players until a single winner remained. Very negative and very short run. Original host: Bill Cullen.

PASSWORD* — CBS 1961

The ultimate word-association game, played between a celebrity and a contestant. Original host: Allen Ludden.

PASSWORD ALL-STARS — ABC 1971

The ultimate word-association game, played between celebrities. Original host: Allen Ludden.

PASSWORD PLUS — NBC 1979

See above above. Original host: Allen Ludden.

PAY CARDS! — Syndication 1968

Games of poker. Original host: Art James.

P.D.Q. — Syndication 1965

Teams of celebs and contestants tried to solve puzzles in the form of phrases. Original host: Dennis James.

PENNY TO A MILLION — ABC 1955

Question one: worth a penny. Subsequent questions doubled the pennies until the game became far from penny-ante. The final round could be worth a million pennies ($10,000). Original host: Bill Goodwin.

PEOPLE ARE FUNNY* — NBC 1954

Contestants were picked from the studio audience and then involved in a "stunt" that proved people really are funny when it comes to decisions that concern things like greed, memory, or self-involvement. A classic. Original host: Art Linkletter.

PEOPLE WILL TALK — NBC 1963

Contestants tried to predict how the studio audience would answer questions. A conceptual forerunner to FAMILY FEUD and THE HOLLYWOOD SQUARES. Original host: Dennis James.

THE PERFECT MATCH — Syndication 1967

A la THE DATING GAME, with a twist. The computer decided who would date who after three prospective couples were interviewed. Original host: Dick Enberg.

THE PERFECT MATCH — Syndication 1986

A la THE NEWLYWED GAME again. More foibles and follies of the recently married. Original host: Bob Goen.

PERSONALITY — NBC 1967

A triple-whammy guess-the-response game. Three celebs took a shot at predicting how each other, the public, and a video-taped celebrity would respond to various questions. Original host: Larry Blyden.

PERSONALITY PUZZLE — ABC 1953

The players were shown personal possessions of three celebrities who were seated behind them. The object was to link the correct possession with the correct celebrity. Original host: Robert Alda.

PERSONALS — NBC 1991

Pretty much the bottom of the game show barrel. The set is a mock singles bar. The audience sits in the bar and watches as beautiful people "arrange" dates by questioning each other about matters explicit ("Do you enjoy a 'trip around the world'?") and inane ("Would you save the ozone layer, if you could?") Viewers call in on a 900 number at a hefty $2.95 per minute to leave messages. The winning couple competes with each other on the "Love Thermometer" section of the show to decide where they are going on their big and sexy date/vacation. Original host: Tim Jones.

Picture This — CBS 1963

Two teams made up of a celebrity and a contestant. One member of the team was given a secret phrase and had to direct an artist to draw in such a way that the other team member could guess it. Original host: Jerry Van Dyke.

Pitfall — Syndication 1981

A show that proved danger lurked everywhere. In the grand finale of this Q & A the player answered questions on a platform that sunk further into the floor for every incorrect answer. Original host: Alex Trebek.

Place the Face — NBC 1953

Contestants met people they hadn't seen for years and had to try to figure out who they were. Original host: Jack Smith.

Play The Game — Dumont 1946

Charades moderated by a very popular NYU professor, from the days when TV's were few and far between. The show was actually produced by ABC so its crews could gain experience for when they had their own studio. Original host: Dr. Harvey Zorbaugh.

Play The Percentages — Syndication 1980

Contestants guessed the percentage of the audience that would answer a question in a certain way. Original host: Geoff Edwards.

Play Your Hunch — CBS 1958

Problem-solving and object-identification game involving teams of related contestants; two brothers, husband and wife, etc. The show hit all three networks from 1958 to 1963 as a daytimer with Robert Q. Lewis and Merv Griffin doing time as hosts. Original host: Johnny Olson.

POP 'N' ROCKER GAME — Syndication 1983

A teen quiz about rock 'n roll. The contestants danced to current hits. Original host: Jon "Bowser" Bauman.

PRESS YOUR LUCK — CBS 1983

A game that taught you not to. Contestants answered questions and received prizes and cash for correct answers. They also earned spins on the big board, where they attempted to stop on squares that represented "big bucks." Lurking with the prize squares were obnoxious little creatures called "whammies." The players could quit at any time and hope they were the money winners but could lose it all if they "pressed their luck" and got "whammied." Original host: Peter Tomarken.

THE PRICE IS RIGHT* — NBC 1956

The venerable and ancient one. The price-setting and guessing game that has survived four decades of TV madness. Original host: Bill Cullen.

PUTTIN' ON THE HITS — Syndication 1985

Contestants lip-synched entire hit songs and advanced to compete for a grand prize of $25,000. Original host: Allen Fawcett.

Q

Q.E.D. — ABC 1951

A crime-solving game in which panelists were shown a short sketch which contained a mystery. The panelists could ask yes or no questions until one of them guessed the solution. Q.E.D. stands for *quod erat demonstrandum*, which means "that which is to be proven." Sometimes the show was called MYSTERY FILE. Original host: Doug Browning.

QUEEN FOR A DAY* — NBC 1956

The classic sobber. Four women with grim and desperate, but marginally light-hearted tales of woe competed for the audience's affection and for merchandise. On the air in one form or another for over 20 years. Original host: Jack Bailey.

QUICK AS A FLASH — ABC 1953

Film shorts produced for the show were presented to a panel which had to guess the outcome. Original host: Bobby Sherwood.

QUICK ON THE DRAW — DUMONT 1952

Cartoonist Bob Dunn drew quickies to suggest certain words or phrases which an ever-changing panel of celebs had to guess. The puns were bad; for example, a comedian taking off his suit was a "comic strip." Original host: Robin Chandler.

QUICKSILVER — USA NETWORK 1994

A USA Network "original." Basic Q & A with this twist. The first round of questions results in eight answers. The second round takes those same eight answers and asks a different set of questions using alternate meanings or word play. The winner gets into the "Silver Streak" where they must pick, in 45 seconds 10 of 15 answers to fit questions from the host. Original host: Ron Maestri.

QUIZ KIDS *— NBC 1949

One of the great transitions from radio to TV. A smart panel of youngsters answered tough questions until 1956. Original host: Jim Kelly.

THE QUIZ KIDS CHALLENGE —Syndication 1990

QUIZ KIDS update. Original host: Jonathan Price.

Quizzing The News — ABC 1948

Another set of training wheels for fledgling ABC. The crews broadcast this current-events quiz out of the competition's studios until their facility was open for business on August 8, 1948. Think that sort of thing would happen today? Original host: Allen Prescott.

R

Reach For The Stars — NBC 1967

Questions and stunts for cash and merchandise. Original host: Bill Mazer.

The Rebus Game — ABC 1965

Four people, two teams, a pad of paper, and a pencil. A draw and guess game. Original host: Jack Linkletter.

The Reel Game — ABC 1971

Contestants placed bets on what they knew about history and events. Period newsreels verified their answers. Original host: Jack Barry.

Remote Control — MTV 1987

A wild and crazy game show for the MTV crowd that also went into syndication in 1989. Original host: Ken Ober.

Rhyme And Reason — ABC 1975

A celebrity panel completed rhymed phrases which were read to contestants who then had to guess which celebrity completed the rhyme. Original host: Bob Eubanks.

Riddle Me This — CBS 1946

The other title for Celebrity Time.

Runaround — NBC 1972

A life-size board game for children. The contestants were asked questions and had to run to squares that contained the right answers. Original host: Paul Winchell.

S

Sale Of The Century — NBC 1969

Quiz that required participants to run to a buzzer when they thought they had the answer. After they built up a chunk of dough, they had a chance to spend it on discounted merchandise. Original host: Jack Kelly.

Sandblast — MTV 1995

Another Gladiators knockoff. Teens go bowling in a swimming pool or play in-your-face, slam dunk basketball off a water tower. Life on the beach for Generation X. Original host: Peter King.

Say It With Acting — NBC 1949

Broadway stars played charades. Original host: Bud Collyer.

Say When! — NBC 1961

The Price Is Right but with a ceiling on how much each contestant could accumulate. If they didn't "say when" before they went over the limit, they lost it all. Original host: Dennis James.

Scrabble — NBC 1984

The famous crossword game on the tube. Clues were given for each word and then contestants chose letters to figure out what it was. The winners were paid in fake money (redeemable) and it was counted out right in front of their eyes by the host. Original host: Chuck Woolery.

SECOND CHANCE — ABC 1977

Contestants were asked a question and given three possible answers. They picked the one they thought was correct and if they were wrong, they got a second chance. Original host: Jim Peck.

SENSE AND NONSENSE — NBC 1953

Contestants were expected to recognize things by their smell, sound, taste, etc. Original host: Bob Kennedy.

SEVEN KEYS — ABC 1961

For every picture identified on the flashy game board, a player got a key. The keys, of course, opened doors to bonus prizes. Original host: Jack Narz.

SHENANIGANS — ABC 1964

Giant board game for youngsters. They moved around according to the roll of giant dice and the first to get off the board won. Original host: Stubby Kaye.

SHOOT FOR THE STARS — NBC 1977

Identify the phrase, win the jackpot. Original host: Geoff Edwards.

SHOP TILL YOU DROP — Syndication 1989

The set was a mock shopping mall in California. The contestants were well-versed in commercial trivia (jingles, ad slogans, brand names). The winners were sent on shopping sprees around the globe.

SHOWDOWN — NBC 1966

In the never-ending struggle to be unique, the penalty for the wrong answer on this otherwise humdrum Q & A was that the chair the contestant was sitting in would break away and spill the chump on the floor. Original host: Joe Pyne.

SHOWOFFS — ABC 1975

Charades again. Original host: Bobby Van.

Sit Or Miss — ABC 1950

Musical chairs the old fashioned way, except that when the contestants lost their chairs, they had to answer a question or perform a stunt. Original co-Hosts: Kay Westfall and George Sotos.

The $64,000 Challenge* — CBS 1956

A spin-off for winners of THE $64,000 QUESTION. They were challenged by contestants and both were asked the same series of questions in a simple elimination process, you miss, you're out. Left the air in its prime when the scandals broke in 1958. Original host: Sonny Fox.

The $64,000 Question* — CBS 1955

Progressively tougher questions for larger and larger amounts of money. The contestants could take their winnings and run at any time. Linked to the big money scandals and canceled abruptly in 1958. Original host: Hal March.

The Sky's The Limit — NBC 1954

From the depths of the studio audience came contestants willing to compete in a Q & A and stunt format. Original host: Monty Hall.

Snap Judgment — NBC 1967

PASSWORD with the clues and responses between team members written on paper. Original host: Ed McMahon.

So You Think You've Got Troubles — Syndication 1982

Participants discussed their problems with Jay and his dummy Bob, after which a panel of experts gave some advice. The participants then had to decide which of the experts the audience agreed with. Original hosts: Jay and Bob.

SPIN-OFF — CBS 1975

Go back and take a look at GIVE-N-TAKE. Original host: Jim Lange.

SPIN THE PICTURE — DUMONT 1949

This pioneering show gave away some pretty large cash prizes for 1949. The first jackpot winner pocketed almost $8,000. The trick was to identify the famous person in a photo that was spinning at great speed or flashed quickly. The show was an hour long and consisted of sketches, music, and drama. Original host: Carl Caruso.

SPLIT PERSONALITY — CBS 1959

Clues led contestants to the identity of a celebrity. Original host: Tom Poston.

SPLIT SECOND* — ABC 1972

A Q & A with the American dream at the end of the road. Winning contestants were given a key to one of five cars. If the key fit, the car was theirs. If not, they could return and try to win again. Original host: Tom Kennedy.

STARCADE — Syndication 1983

Children competed in video games on television. The cream of the crop won cash and prizes. Original host: Geoff Edwards.

STOP ME IF YOU'VE HEARD THIS ONE — ABC 1948

Viewers sent in jokes which were read to a panel of comics. If one of the comics got the punch line before the joke was finished, he yelled "Stop!" If he was right, the viewer got nothing; if he was wrong, the viewer won a prize. Original host: Roger Bower.

Stop The Music* — ABC 1949

The first of the musical guessing games. Inspired by a gimmick used by band leader Harry Salter when he was on tour. He would play snatches of a tune and the listeners would yell, "Stop the Music!" when they knew the answer. Original host: Bert Parks.

Storybook Squares — NBC 1968

Children's version of The Hollywood Squares with the tic-tac-toe board filled with story book characters. Original host: Peter Marshall.

Strike It Rich*— CBS 1951

People brought their tales of woe to the studio audience and answered simple questions for cash to bail themselves out. Original host: Warren Hull.

Studs — Fox 1989

Three women, two guys. The guys choose two of the gals to take on dates. Number three is out in the cold. The couples return to discuss the dates and the women judge which of the guys is the "biggest stud." Lots of innuendo and leering, with some of the best lines reportedly supplied by the show's writers. Original host: Mark DeCarlo.

Stump The Stars

The other name for Pantomime Quiz.

Stumpers! — NBC 1976

Another variation on Password that allowed the teams of celebrities and regular folks to use three-word clues instead of one. Original host: Allen Ludden.

Super Ghost — NBC 1952

Like the parlor game of old, three panelists tried to avoid completing words on their blackboard. Three completions and they "disappeared." Original host: Dr. Bergen Evans.

Super Password — NBC 1984

Password for bigger bucks. Original host: Bert Convy

Super Jeopardy! — ABC 1990

Like the name says. Original host: Alex Trebek

Supermarket Sweep — ABC 1965

You tear down the aisle of a supermarket with a basket or cart and you have a specified amount of time to fill it up with expensive items. The winner grabbed the most. Original host: Bill Malone.

T

Tag The Gag — NBC 1950

Because it lasted just two weeks, this Q & A in which comics attempted to guess punch lines had no impact at all. Original host: Hal Block.

Take a Chance — NBC 1950

Simple and good natured Q & A in which contestants could build their winnings or "take a chance" and quit while they were ahead. Original host: Don Ameche.

Take a Good Look — ABC 1959

Maybe this is where Andy Worhol got his "15 minutes of fame" concept. Each contestant on the show had a short burst of notoriety and it was the panelists' job to guess their identity. Original host: Ernie Kovacs.

Take a Guess — CBS 1953

An object was placed on stage and the contestants had the incentive to quickly guess what it was because they lost money from their stash each time they had to ask a question. Original host: John Caffery.

Take Two — ABC 1963

A similar element existed in each of four pictures shown to contestants. The winner guessed what it was. Original host: Don McNeil.

Tattletales — CBS 1974

An updated version of He Said, She Said. Original host: Bert Convy.

Temptation —ABC 1967

Q & A with the usual lure of larger prizes if the contestant wanted to continue playing. Original host: Art James.

The $10,000 Pyramid* — CBS 1973

Word-association game with a celebrity/contestant team. Fast action and lots of glitz. Original host: Dick Clark.

That's Amore — Syndication 1992

Couples who have been together or married for what must seem like eons get a chance to bicker with each other on the air and let the audience decide who's in the right.

Think Fast — ABC 1949

Panelists tried to outlast each other talking about things given to them by the host. Original host: Dr. Mason Gross.

Three For The Money -- NBC 1975

The hook for this Q & A was that, just like a regular job, the contestants were on the show for a whole week. The difference was that only the winner collected a paycheck on Friday. Original host: Dick Enberg.

Three on a Match — NBC 1971

True/False Q & A with a prize-board round for the winner. Original host: Bill Cullen.

Three's a Crowd — Syndication 1979

Newlywed Game spin-off with the central issue being who knew more about the husband—his wife or his secretary. Scary. Original host: Jim Peck.

Tic Tac Dough — NBC 1956

The big board was the familiar squared layout and contestants got Xs or Os for correct answers. The show had a decent run on network and in syndication. Win Elliot was the host for the entire nighttime run of the show after the premier episode. Original host: Jay Jackson.

The Time Machine — NBC 1985

Nostalgia and trivia were the subject of this Q & A. Original host: John Davidson.

Time Will Tell — Dumont 1954

The contestants tried to come up with one-word answers to silly questions. The one who answered the most questions in 90 seconds won. Original host: Ernie Kovacs.

To Say The Least — NBC 1977

Celebrities competed to get their point across with the fewest words or guesses. Original host: Tom Kennedy.

To Tell The Truth* — CBS 1956

Three contestants, all pretending to be the same person, were questioned by the panel as they attempted to guess which contestant was actually who they purported to be. Original host: Bud Collyer.

Top Dollar — CBS 1958

A word game played on a large board. The contestants actually did what was later to make Vanna White famous, they placed letters on the board to try to guess a word before using up all the letters needed to complete it. Original host: Toby Reed.

TOP OF THE WORLD — PBS 1982

A high-class Q & A with an international flavor on public television. Contestants from different countries competed using their knowledge of general subjects. Original host: Eamonn Andrews.

TREASURE HUNT* — ABC 1956

A man and a woman were picked from the studio audience and paired up to answer questions. The winner went on a frenzied search for treasure hidden on the stage. When the show returned under the wing of Chuck Barris, the Q & A part was cut and the participants simply engaged in a frenzied search for the treasure. Original host: Geoff Edwards.

TREASURE ISLE — ABC 1967

Take the frenzied search for merchandise and prizes outside and place it in a lagoon on an island off the coast of Florida. Greed and sun—a perfect combo. Original host: John Bartholomew Tucker.

TREASURE QUEST — ABC 1949

If you guessed the location, you got to go there, all expenses paid. Original host: John Weigel.

TRIVIA TRAP — ABC 1984

Reverse trivia. The trick was to guess which of the answers was wrong. Original host: Bob Eubanks.

TRUTH OR CONSEQUENCES* — CBS 1950

If you can't answer the stupid question, you have to perform the stupid stunt. The great one, it became a cottage industry for its crerators and producers running through four decades. Original host: Ralph Edwards.

Twenty–One* — NBC 1956

The questions were tough, the money was huge (top prize $252,000 , won by a man named Teddy Nadler). Unfortunately, however, the game was rigged. The scandal brought down an American icon, Charles Van Doren. Original host: Jack Barry.

Twenty Questions* — NBC 1949

The ancient parlor game brought to the tube. Panelists had twenty yes or no questions to guess the object. The first question was always "Is it animal, mineral, or vegetable?" Original host: Bill Slater.

The $25,000 Pyramid — Syndication 1974

Up the pyramid prize a cool fifteen grand. Original host: Bill Cullen.

The $20,000 Pyramid — ABC 1976

The original concept, adjusted for inflation. Original host: Dick Clark

Two For The Money — NBC 1952

Round one: two teams competed for cash in a Q & A. Round two: The same teams competed for cash in a Q & A. Original host: Herb Shriner.

Two In Love — CBS 1954

Friends and family of recently engaged, newly married, or couples celebrating a wedding anniversary competed in a friendly fashion to answer questions about the loved ones relationship. Correct answers put cash in the couple's "nest egg." Original host: Bert Parks.

U

Up To Paar — NBC 1952

Five members of the studio audience were selected by Jack and quizzed on current events. They got silver dollars for correct answers, but wrong answers put the dollars in the Jackpot. At the end of the game, the players competed for the pot by writing down their answers to a common question on a piece of paper. Original host: Jack Paar.

V

Video Village* — CBS 1960

Breakthrough game because the producers used the technology of television for the first time to create a total environment (The Video Village) in which contestants competed for prizes. Original host: Jack Narz.

W

Way Out Games — CBS 1976

Stunt-oriented event for teenagers. Usually out of doors, usually centered on athletic skill. Original host: Sonny Fox.

We Take Your Word — CBS 1950

A panel attempted to define and chart the history of words submitted by viewers. The prize for stumping the panel was $50. Original host: John McCaffery.

What Do You Have In Common? — CBS 1954

Three contestants chosen because they all had something in common quizzed each other to find out what it was. The first one to figure it out won $500. Original host: Ralph Story.

What Happened? — NBC 1952

Contestants were folks who had had something happen to them that made them newsworthy. It was up to the panel to figure out what that was. Original host: Ben Grauer.

What Happens Now?

The other title for The Ad-Libbers.

What In The World? — CBS 1953

Set in the University of Pennsylvania Museum, this show quizzed three experts on the works and objects displayed. The only game show to win the Peabody Award for journalism. Original host: Dr. Froelich Rainey.

What's Going On? — ABC 1954

Six celebrities were divided into two groups. One group stayed in the studio and the other went to an undisclosed location. It was the job of the group in the studio to figure out where the other group was and what was going on. Original host: Lee Bowman.

What's In A Word? — CBS 1954

A word-association panel show in which contestants made up two-word rhymes like "Major Cager" or "Nice Rice" and the panel, which was given the noun portion, had to guess the adjective. Original host: Clifton Fadiman.

What's It For? — NBC 1957

Inventors in the spotlight. Oddball inventions were presented to the panel along with the creative thinker who conceived them. The panelists asked questions to figure out what the object was and what it did. Original host: Hal March.

WHAT'S MY LINE?* — CBS 1950

A prime example of simple is good. The panel of witty and interesting people questioned contestants in order to guess their occupations. The show ran for over 17 years. Original host: John Daly.

WHAT'S MY NAME? — NBC 1952

Identify the famous personality from clues given by the host and win a savings bond. Original hosts: ventriloquist Paul Winchell and his dummy Jerry Mahoney.

WHAT'S THE STORY? — DUMONT 1951

Current-events quiz with a panel of media experts. Evidently pretty boring, but for some reason, the show ran until 1955. It has the distinction of being the last program that wasn't boxing to be aired on the dying Dumont Network. Original host: Walt Raney.

WHAT'S THIS SONG? — NBC 1964

Just in case things aren't obscure enough, what about a show where you would have to know the *second* chorus of a song in order to be able to play? Original host: Wink Martindale.

WHAT'S YOUR BID? — ABC 1953

The studio audience came to the show with their own money to bid on merchandise. If they went over the retail price, they got more stuff. All the proceeds went to charity. It didn't matter much because the concept of spending instead of winning at a game show just didn't wash with most folks. Original host: Robert Alda.

WHEEL OF FORTUNE — CBS 1953

That's right. There was another one. The wheel was spun in this game to determine the reward good Samaritans or heroes would receive for their good works. And it offered the possibility of a $1,000 jackpot bonus, proving that it pays to be good. Original host: Todd Russell.

Wheel Of Fortune* — NBC 1975

The one and only. Contestants spin a wheel that determines the value of letters that are placed on the board by the beautiful Vanna White. The letters make a phrase, and the first to guess it is a winner. Pat Sajak is the main man and has been for years. But... Original host: Chuck Wollery.

Where In The World Is Carmen Sandiego? — PBS 1992

It takes a solid knowledge of geography and some serious sleuthing ability to catch up to Carmen and her gang on this award winning children's show. Original host: Greg Lee.

Where Was I? — Dumont 1952

Words and photographs gave clues to a location. The panel had to figure out where the location was. Original host: Dan Seymour.

Whew! — CBS 1979

Breakneck speed was the hook for this one. Two contestants answered rapid-fire Q & A and tried to block opponents from completing their path on the game board. Original host: Tom Kennedy.

Who Do You Trust?

The other title for Do You Trust Your Wife?

Whodunit? — NBC 1979

The old mystery unfolds before the panel of experts and contestants but stops just short of revealing "whodunit." Who can solve the crime first? Real cops interviewed the "suspects" and F. Lee Bailey was a panelist. Original host: Ed McMahon.

Who Pays? — NBC 1959

Three panelists put their heads together to figure out which public figure or other famous person paid the salary of the contestants. The game was played in two rounds of questioning with the money doubling if the panelists couldn't guess after the first round. Original host: Mike Wallace.

Who Said That? — NBC 1948

Viewers sent in quotes from current newspapers, and it was up to the panel of newsmen and celebrities to match the quote with the newsmaker. If they couldn't, the viewer won cash. If the quote came from the producer, the money went to charity. Original host: Robert Trout.

Who, What, or Where Game — NBC 1969

A test of common knowledge with questions that started with (surprise!) who, what, or where. Original host: Art James.

Who's The Boss? — ABC 1954

Celebrities' secretaries were in the spotlight on this one. The panel asked questions to figure out who the big deal was. The secretaries made money for stumping the panel. Mike "Myron" Wallace took over the show midway through the run. Original host: Walter Kiernan.

Who's There? — CBS 1952

Panel attempted to identify a famous person by taking a look a pieces of clothing or objects that were linked to them. Original host: Arlene Francis.

Whose Whose? — CBS 1951

This show has the distinction of having a one-broadcast run. We can gather that viewers weren't interested in watching people guess who was married to whom. Original host: Phil Baker.

WHY? — ABC 1953

A panel of regular people from a broad spectrum of American life were given the who, where, and when of a given situation. They had to figure out the why. Original host: Bill Cullen.

WILD WEST SHOWDOWN — Syndication 1995

More fantasy and brutal gladiator-type fun, old-west style. Wearing hats and boots, contestants live out their dreams of rousting the bad guys and getting the girl or whatever.

WIN, LOSE, OR DRAW — NBC 1987

Two teams composed of two celebs and a regular person. The player attempted to communicate a phrase to teammates by drawing it. Burt Reynolds originated the idea and was often on the show. As a matter of fact, the set looked like his living room. Original host: Bert Convy.

WIN WITH A WINNER — NBC 1958

A horse-race gambling game in which the players were the horses. Each correct answer to a question moved them closer to the finish line. Original host: Sandy Becker.

WIN WITH THE STARS — Syndication 1968

Identify the tune first, win money. Let your celebrity partner help you out. Original host: Allen Ludden.

WINNER TAKE ALL* — CBS 1948

A Q & A noted mostly for its firsts: the first buzzer and the first to let winners defend their title and have a chance to win more cash. Original host: Bud Collyer.

WINGO — CBS 1958

A Q & A with a top prize of $25,000 during the Wingo section, which was a chaotic word game where the player attempted to spell Wingo on the big board. It lasted about a month. Original host: Tom Kennedy.

WINNING STREAK — NBC 1974

The correct answers to general-knowledge questions bought letters which the contestants used to make words to win cash. Original host: Bill Cullen.

WITH THIS RING — DUMONT 1951

Couples who were recently engaged would answer questions on the show about how they would handle the kinds of situations sure to confront them in married life. Married judges evaluated the answers, and the happy couples got trips and prizes for saying the right things. Original host: Bill Slater.

THE WIZARD OF ODDS — NBC 1973

Odds and averages were the meat of this guessing game, as in "How many Americans go to France every year?" Original host: Alex Trebek.

WORD FOR WORD — NBC 1963

A big word appeared on the game board. Contestants scored for every little word they could cull from it. Original host: Merv Griffin.

WORDPLAY — NBC 1986

A dictionary-definition game for celebrities. Original host: Tom Kennedy.

WORDS AND MUSIC — NBC 1970

Clues to a phrase or person were hidden in song lyrics. Original host: Wink Martindale.

Did You Know That...

Pee Wee Herman launched his comedic career on THE GONG SHOW.

X

The Xavier Cugat Show — NBC 1957

No, no, Xavier didn't have a game show. He had a Latin big-band show with his torchy wife, Abby Lane. We just wondered if you were paying attention. He did appear on The $64,000 Question. He *was* called to testify before the congressional committee investigating the rigging of the big-money game shows in 1959. It's also nice to have an X in a compendium like this.

Y

You Bet Your Life* — NBC 1950

This Q & A in name only was a vehicle for Groucho Marx to exercise his wit and acerbic humor. Two contestants from the studio audience, matched for their obvious comic potential, tried to answer simple questions or just get a word in edgewise. The eleven-year run was television wackiness at its best. Original and only host: Groucho Marx.

You Don't Say* — NBC 1963

The missing word in sentences was the team member's clue to the identity of a famous person. "It's what you don't say that counts." Original host: Tom Kennedy.

Your First Impression — NBC 1962

More mystery guests. Who are they? Original host: Bill Leyden.

Your Lucky Clue — CBS 1952

Solve the crime using tricky and devious clues. The twist? Sherlock himself was on the case. Original host: Basil Rathbone.

YOUR NUMBER'S UP — NBC 1985

Contestants completed phrases which, in turn, formed the answers to questions. For each correct answer a number was posted on the board until seven digits were shown. If a home viewer had the phone number represented by the digits, they could call in and win too. Original host: Nipsy Russell.

YOUR SURPRISE PACKAGE — CBS 1961

A Q & A in which contestants competed for a surprise package of cash and prizes. Original host: George Fenneman.

YOUR SURPRISE STORE — CBS 1952

A simple Q & A. The winner got merchandise. The maker of the merchandise got publicity. It's how television works. Original host: Lew Parker.

YOURS FOR A SONG — ABC 1961

The song has missing lyrics. Fill them in and win. Original host: Bert Parks.

YOU'RE IN THE PICTURE* — CBS 1961

The show was canceled after one broadcast because no one, especially The Great One, was interested in watching panelists try to guess the nature of the cardboard cutouts they were sticking their heads through. Original host: Jackie Gleason (who went on the air the second week to cancel the show in person).

YOU'RE ON YOUR OWN — CBS 1956

The stage of the studio was littered with information in the form of reference materials and books. Contestants could use anything they wanted to come up with answers. The prize: up to $25,000. Original host: Steve Dunne.

MAY WE HAVE THE DEFINITIONS PLEASE!

28

A Game Show Glossary
With a Little Tongue in Cheek

ANNOUNCER

The mysterious person with the deep, resonant, or strange voice who introduces the show's host, tells us how exciting the next period of time in our lives will be and describes to us in great detail the nature of the merchandise or the amount of cash the contestant has just won or lost. He also says goodbye and tells us how to get on the show. Announcers are usually chained in studio basements and released only for tapings.

AUTHORITY

A gentleman or woman or group of gentlemen or women who inspire respect and confidence because of their enormous intellect and the fact that they own their own encyclopedias. The Authority is on hand to settle disputes about answers and to make everyone feel that someone is in charge. The Authority used to be responsible for protecting the answers on shows like TWENTY-ONE by doing things like keeping them in bank vaults or a CPA's office. Clearly the idea didn't work out so well and nobody bothers with it much any more.

BIG-MONEY SHOW

A genre of game show, usually Q & A, in which contestants pit their skills or memory and intelligence against one another for amazingly large sums of money. Big-Money Shows have intellectual content and require the presence of the Authority to insure accuracy.

BUZZER

The annoyingly loud sound that alerts the contestant and the host that their time is up. The buzzer is the single element, with the exception of the host and a clock, that no game show can do without. The buzzer is often given cute names such as Beulah, but no matter what it's called, it strikes terror into the heart of a sweating contestant.

CASH

Why one aspires to get on a game show. As in, "I want to win some cash, Bob!"(*See* Winner.) Also a singer named Johnny's last name.

CELEBRITY

A celebrity is any public person, great or near-great, so designated by the producer or the host of a game show. Whether or not anyone in the studio audience has heard of the celebrity is immaterial. Once a person has been designated a celebrity by a producer or host he retains the title until death, after which he becomes merely famous. Celebrities can also be women, in which case the requisite pronouns would be *she* or *her*.

CHAMPION

The champion on a game show is more than a winner. The champion is an icon and a model of success to be envied and respected. Champions can retain their title by quitting while they're on top or risk it all by continuing to play. (*see* Loser.)

CLOCK

The clock keeps track of the amount of time a contestant has to complete a task or answer a question. It can be seen or unseen. The clock either ticks loudly or is represented by irritating music which is used to keep the pressure on the contestant. The clock also functions as a means to keep the host awake.

CONCEPT

An idea for a game show. As in "Bob, I've got a concept! We'll hide the prize in a basket." All game shows have concepts, the good ones tend to make sense.

CONNECTION SHOW

Game show where the concept is to put people of the opposite sex (usually) who don't know each other particularly well, preferably not at all, into intimate situations, and then get them to talk about it all on national television. Usually preceded by the word LOVE, but can be a combination of the words, DATING and GAME or even single words such as PERSONALS, INFATUATION, or STUDS. If the relationship is a success the couple has the potential of moving to the next level. (*See* Couple-Baiting Show.)

CONSOLATION PRIZE

What a contestant gets for being a loser. A consolation prize is not desired by people with competitive natures and is usually accepted with brave and/or teary smiles that are tinged with envy.

CONTESTANT

A grown person or child or whoever, with the courage to go on national television and play a game of skill and/or intelligence for a reward of cash and/or merchandise. Most normal people don't want to do this because the prospect of embarrassment and humiliation before millions of viewers is not pleasing.

Couple-Baiting Show

A show in which teams of couples—newly married, engaged, recently parents, or recently divorced—show how much they know or don't know about each other by how they respond to questions about their personal and intimate moments. Although there are prizes, the main purpose of a couple-baiting show is to provoke arguments, disagreements, misunderstandings, and fistfights, and to promote sexual hilarity in general. As in (your choice) The _____ Game (Newlywed, New Newlywed, New New Newlywed, etc.).

Disclaimer

What the announcer says whenever the sponsor, producer, or network lawyers feel that something might be misunderstood or needs to be clarified, such as the winner will be paid over a period of 40 years. The disclaimer usually appears at the end of the show. The print is usually very small and the announcer speaks very fast as in automobile leasing commercials.

Envelope

The sealed paper sleeve that holds secret and important information such as questions or prize information or the host's ad-libs.

Fun

What winners have. (See also No Fun.)

Game

A competition between individuals or teams with specific rules of play. A game is played for the amusement and simple fun of those who participate and is considered a diversion. And if you believe that...

GAME BOARD

A graphic representation of the contestant's progress in the game. The game board should be overbearing and filled with high-tech bells and whistles. It should also look like it cost a lot of money.

GONG

A large brass plate with a booming and intrusive sound that alerts a contestant on a Chuck Barris production to the fact that they've failed. Not to be confused with the gorilla from the old movie.

GUEST

A guest is someone who comes into your home for a visit or appears on a game show. A guest can be a celebrity or just a normal person with obsessive ambition.

GUEST HOST

A person of some stature who emcees a game show when the regular host doesn't want to.

HOST

A person who can't believe how lucky he is to get this great job that is pretty easy and results in large bank accounts along with free clothes.

HOSTESS

A person who can't believe how lucky she is to get this great job that is pretty easy and results in large bank accounts along with free clothes. Hostesses were more common in the days before neutral gender.

LIGHTNING ROUND

A section near the end of a game show that has many clever names (Jackpot, Final Jeopardy! etc.) and is the reward for succeeding. It is noted for its difficulty and the tension-producing elements that accompany it such as flashing lights and loud music.

LIVE

What happens on television when the tape breaks. It used to happen all the time.

LIVE ON TAPE

This is too difficult a philosophical and metaphysical question to deal with in a book called the *TV Game Show Almanac*.

LOSER

Someone who has failed miserably on a game show in front of millions of people and has to content himself with a consultation prize such as three cases of Draino instead of $400,000.

MERCHANDISE

Whatever the sponsor wants to give away instead of cash. Presentations of merchandise are usually accompanied by a lengthy description by the announcer while everyone smiles.

MYSTERY GUEST

A guest whose identity is not revealed until the panel has asked a lot of probing questions. Sometimes the mystery guest is still a mystery even after their name has been revealed.

NO FUN

What losers have no matter what they say.

ON TAPE

Why a producer can do a full week of game shows in one day.

PANEL SHOW

A game show in which guests, who are by their nature (or by producers definition) celebrities, sit behind a long desk and either guess or judge. Their prime function, however, is to chat and be witty. Not to be confused with breakfast panel meeting about productivity at an aluminum siding convention.

PANELIST

A single celebrity element of a panel.

PIZZAZZ

A major part of a game show concept. As in... "But does it have pizzazz, Bob?"

PLUNGER

An object at a contestant's station, usually large and red. It is used by the contestant to signal to the host that an answer is imminent. Also called a button or a knob or that thing you push before the other guy does so as to beat him.

PRIZE

What a contestant gets for defeating his opponent.

PRIZE MODEL

A beautiful young person, almost always female, used to make the merchandise offered on a game show look great or at least better than it actually is.

PRODUCER

Someone with a concept who knows a friend of a guy high up in the network. Producers tend to look busy and nervous. They also tend to be looking over their shoulders to see who's gaining on them.

QUIZ

A series of questions which need answers. What did you think it was?

ROUND

A section of a game show that has a beginning, middle and end, just like *Hamlet*. Except in game shows, contestants move to the next round for being right instead of having to suck it up and kill their uncle for revenge.

SECRET WORD

Are you kidding, we're not going to just *tell* you that.

SET

The fantastical palace where a game show takes place. The set is in a studio and put together by stagehands who could care less about what takes place on it. A set is usually so garish that most people would not want one in their homes.

SOB-STORY SHOW

Contestants on sob or agony shows are noted for their desperation and willingness to share their failures and sadness in exchange for cash or merchandise. (*See* QUEEN FOR A DAY and STRIKE IT RICH).

SPONSOR

Someone with a product who believes against all logic that advertising works.

STAR

A celebrity or a host who believes his own press.

STRATEGY

The plan of attack people who are about to become contestants on a game show devise in order to win big bucks. The plan usually involves watching the show a lot and trying to imagine whether or not the lights are really as hot as they look and if the host really dyes his hair. There have been cases where people watched the show a lot, actually learned what to do, and hit the jackpot. *See* Chapter 18.

STUDIO AUDIENCE

A group of people who gather together to watch a game show taping for free. They are usually on vacation or have nothing else to do. Sometimes members of the studio audience are chosen to participate in a game show, if so, they automatically become a guest and have the opportunity to become a celebrity, star, or host.

STUNT SHOW

The ultimate in public humiliation in exchange for cash or merchandise. Producers who studied with the Marquis de Sade invent weird and difficult tasks that require a strange range of skills to complete. Contestants go in with their eyes wide open and do their best. Stunt shows are fun.

TEST

What an aspiring contestant takes and has to pass in order to be considered for a game show. Since that mess in the 50s, the producers are reluctant to include the answers with the test.

TIMER

The person hired by the producer to push the buzzer when a contestant fails. The timer is considered a minor authority only because he wields power. (*See also* Clock).

TRAINING SESSION

What contestants go through with the production team before the show so that they will appear natural and at home, even if they are scared to death.

TREND

What producers try to get ahead of when they think up game shows so they won't have to stand in line at the network door, as in "We're ahead of the trend on this one, Bob!"

VIEWERS AT HOME

You and me, babe (and millions of others).

WARM UP

The part of the game show that precedes the actual game. During this time a person who usually thinks he's funnier than he actually is tells amusing anecdotes to make the audience laugh. He also shows them the applause meter and tells them how to respond to it using both hands. The warm up can sometimes go on for hours if the host is in a funk and won't come out of his dressing room. (*See also* Guest Host).

WINNER

The person we all aspire to be, the person with the right answer at the right time. (*See also* Fun).

Something for Everyone

A local cable station in New York City occasionally airs a show called THE GAY DATING GAME. The lucky couple gets tickets for the Circle Line boat ride around the island of Manhattan. The hosts are a leather queen and a transvestite.

QUIZ ANSWERS

274

Answers to Quiz 1: Part One

1. 22 (Term limits on the Presidency passed in 1951)
2. Africa
3. Lucky Lady II
4. Eight
5. August Rodin
6. 1863
7. Ted Williams
8. a) winner had 14
   b) winner had 5
   c) winner had 17
9. I Was a Communist for the FBI
10. Callander

Lightning Round

If your answer is yes, you would have raked in $22,400 on ABC's STOP THE MUSIC.

Answers to Quiz 1: Part Two

1. 12 O'Clock High
2. *Mona Lisa*
3. Billy the Kid
4. Leon Cadore (Brooklyn) and Joe Osechger (Boston)
5. Falstaff
6. a) winner had 17
   b) winner had 7
   c) winner had 10
7. Ambrosia
8. Tripolitan
9. Napoleon Bonaparte (Rip took a "nap")
10. Gaul

Lightning Round

If your answer is yes, you would have cleaned up $35,250 on ABC's STOP THE MUSIC.

Answers to Quiz 2

1. sportscaster
2. actor
3. comedian/joke writer
4. actor/comedian
5. syndicated cartoonist (*Li'l Abner*)
6. talk show host (*The Tonight Show*)
7. book editor
8. pro baseball catcher/sportscaster
9. Broadway writer/director/author
10. comedian/ writer
11. stripper
12. humorist
13. actor/cookbook writer
14. actor
15. sportscaster
16. newscaster
17. newscaster (Mike Wallace of *60 Minutes*)
18. ventriloquist
19. pro football linebacker
20. editor
21. actor
22. baseball manager
23. country and gospel singer
24. Olympic gold medalist
25. Miss America
26. actor
27. writer/director
28. actor
29. Broadway dancer/actor
30. comedian
31. Broadway actor/comedian

Answers to Quiz 3: Part One.

1. Mike Wallace hosted THE BIG SURPRISE, GUESS AGAIN, I'LL BUY THAT, WHO PAYS, WHO'S THE BOSS. Under his real first name, Myron, he hosted MAJORITY RULES.
2. Minnesota Fats.
3. Female pro Billy Jean King.
4. Lee Trevino, golfer;
   Bruce Jenner, Olympic gold medalist;
   Joe Garagiola, baseball player.
5. Called "The Commissioner" on Star Games, all-pro hall-of-famer Butkus played linebacker for the Chicago Bears and was considered one of the best to ever play the game.

6. *This Is Your Life*.
7. Marlon Brando.
8. Jackie Gleason (YOU'RE IN THE PICTURE). He considered the show so bad that he apologized to the viewing audience on live television and promised they would never be subjected to this particular show again.
9. Jay Wolpert of Glen Cove, New York.

Answers to Quiz 3: Part Two

1. James Dean.
2. Walter Cronkite, IT'S NEWS TO ME;
   Mike Wallace, THE BIG SURPRISE;
   Ben Grauer, SAY IT WITH ACTING;
   John Cameron Swayzee, CHANCE FOR ROMANCE;
   Robert Trout, WHO SAID THAT?
3. Johnny Mercer.
4. THE NEIGHBORS (host);
   ALMOST ANYTHING GOES (interviewer).
5. Jacqueline Susann.
6. Dick (LAUGH LINE, MOTHER'S DAY) VanDyke
   Jerry (PICTURE THIS) Van Dyke.
7. Edgar Bergen, DO YOU TRUST YOUR WIFE?;
   Paul Winchell, RUNAROUND.
8. Mel Blanc.
9. The Freddy Martin Orchestra.
   The CBS Morning Show.
   The Robert Q. Lewis Show.

Answers to Quiz 3: Part Three

1. Dick Cavett, COLLEGE BOWL '87;
   Merv Griffin, KEEP TALKING,
      PLAY YOUR HUNCH,
      WORD FOR WORD.

2. Milton Caniff.
3. Leo Durocher.
4. Phyllis George.
5. FUN FOR THE MONEY.
6. Joe Garagiola (baseball) and Lynn Swann (football).
7. Louis Untermeyer of WHAT'S MY LINE?.
8. Buddy Hackett and Bill Cosby.
9. WHAT'S MY LINE, TO TELL THE TRUTH, and I'VE GOT A SECRET.

Answers to Quiz 4

1. DOTTO, NBC 1958; Jack Narz.
2. Ed blew the whistle on the rigging of game shows
   when he found a notebook backstage belonging to
   a DOTTO winner. The notebook contained answers
   to questions she had been asked on the previous
   show. He brought it to the attention of the losing contestant,
   and when they confronted the producers
   they were offered a payoff. When Ed found out that
   he had gotten less money than his partner, he
   contacted the Attorney General's office in
   Manhattan, and the rest is history.
3. Dr. Joyce Brothers won $64,000.
4. CONCENTRATION was intended to be a temporary replacement
   and was hosted for a short time by Jack Barry, who had run
   TWENTY-ONE.
5. The Hon. Oren Harris of Washington.
6. INVESTIGATION OF TELEVISION QUIZ SHOWS
   HEARINGS
   BEFORE A
   SUBCOMMITTEE OF THE
   COMMITTEE ON
   INTERSTATE AND FOREIGN COMMERCE
   HOUSE OF REPRESENTATIVES
   EIGHTY-SIXTH CONGRESS
7. Staten Island cop Redmond O'Hanlon who pocketed $8,000.

8. In September of 1955, Richard McCutcheon, a captain in the U.S. Marines, won for his expertise in food and cooking.
9. Revlon; Demand for Living lipstick.
10. He turned up the heat in the isolation booths so the folks would perspire as they concentrated.
11. Richard Jackman. He refused to go along.
12. Herb Stempel. They dressed him up as an ex-GI. The problem was that the producers didn't think he had the moxie to maintain viewer interest. After a few weeks they told him he had to throw the game to Charles Van Doren. It turned out to be a big mistake.
13. $49,000; he also received an up-front payment of $18,500.
14. The "Wizard of Quiz."
15. The magazine was *Life*'s alter ego, *Look*.
16. The *New York Journal American,* the *World-Telegram* and the *Sun*. The story appeared in the editions of August 28, 1958.
17. Patty Duke.
18. President Frank Stanton immediately canceled every show on his network that gave away cash or prizes.
19. $4,500 per year.
20. THE JOKER'S WILD on CBS.
21. They said that they were doing it to entertain the viewing audience and make the show more exciting.
22. VIDEO VILLAGE (1960).
23. Monty Hall. Canada.

Answers to Quiz 5

You need more than an answer to a quiz if you're really looking here.

Answers to Quiz 6

1. DOTTO, NBC 1958.
   DROODLES, NBC 1954.
   DRAW TO WIN, CBS 1952.
2. Denis Darcel was the hostess of GAMBLE ON LOVE.
3. PASSWORD ALL-STARS, PASSWORD PLUS, SUPER PASSWORD.
4. $20,000,$25,000, $50,000, $100,000 PYRAMID.
5. DETECTO anticipated TO TELL THE TRUTH,
   THINK ALIKE anticipated THE NEWLYWED GAME,
   WHAT'S MY OCCUPATION? anticipated WHAT'S MY LINE?,
   WHAT'S IN THE BOX? anticipated LET'S MAKE A DEAL.
6. STOP THE MUSIC! and NAME THAT TUNE!
7. STORYBOOK SQUARES was based on
   THE HOLLYWOOD SQUARES.
   The host was, of course, Peter Marshall.
8. BLIND DATE was hosted by Arlene Francis.

Answers to Quiz 7

A 6
B 9
C 7
D 1
E 4
F 8
G 10
H 2
I 5
J 3